The GOD-MAN

Christ in the Gospels

PositiveAction
BIBLE CURRICULUM

The God-Man: Christ in the Gospels
STUDENT MANUAL

Written by Cherie Noel

Copyright © 1993, 2014 by Positive Action for Christ, Inc., P.O. Box 700, 502 West Pippen Street, Whitakers, NC 27891.

www.positiveaction.org

Second Edition 2014
First Printing

Printed in the United States of America

ISBN: 978-1-59557-190-8

Edited by Steve Braswell and David Gambrell
Design by Shannon Brown

Published by

CONTENTS

Lesson 1: The Eternal Christ 7

Lesson 2: The Prophetic Christ 13

Lesson 3: The Birth and Childhood of Christ 19

Lesson 4: John the Baptist, the Forerunner of Christ . . . 27

Lesson 5: The Temptation of Christ 33

Lesson 6: Three Important Firsts 39

Lesson 7: Nicodemus Finds Jesus 45

Lesson 8: Judea, Samaria, Galilee 51

Lesson 9: Jesus Ordains His Disciples 57

Lesson 10: The Year of Popularity 63

Lesson 11: The Sermon on the Mount (Part 1) 69

Lesson 12: The Sermon on the Mount (Part 2) 75

Lesson 13: Jesus, the Master Teacher 81

Lesson 14: The Deity of Jesus Christ 87

Lesson 15: Growing Opposition 93

Lesson 16: Jesus, the Bread of Life 101

Lesson 17: Review 107

Lesson 18: The Mighty Works of Jesus 115

Lesson 19: Confusion and Division Concerning Jesus . 121

Lesson 20: Lessons on Humility 127

Lesson 21: Lessons on Forgiveness 133

Lesson 22: The True Meaning of Love 139

Lesson 23: Analogies of Christ 145

Lesson 24: The Raising of Lazarus 151

Lesson 25: "The Fullness of the Time" Had Come 157

Lesson 26: The Triumphal Entry 163

Lesson 27: Days of Conflict 169

Lesson 28: Final Warnings 175

Lesson 29: The Last Passover 181

Lesson 30: Last Words and Promises 187

Lesson 31: Betrayal and Trials 191

Lesson 32: The Day Christ Died 201

Lesson 33: The Resurrection 205

Lesson 34: The Ascension 211

Lesson 35: Review 215

THE GOD-MAN SCRIPTURE MEMORIZATION REPORT SHEET

Name: _____ Grade: _____ Teacher: _____

Week	Scripture	Due Date	Parent's Signature
1	John 1:1–2		
2	John 1:3–5		
3	John 1:6–7		
4	John 1:8–10		
5	John 1:11–12		
6	John 1:13–14		
7	John 1:1–14		
8	Proverbs 3:1–2		
9	Proverbs 3:3–4		
10	Proverbs 3:5–6		
11	Proverbs 3:7–8		
12	Proverbs 3:9–10		
13	Proverbs 3:11–13		
14	Proverbs 3:1–13		
15	Galatians 6:1–3		
16	Galatians 6:4–6		
17	Galatians 6:7–8		
18	Galatians 6:9–10		
19	Galatians 6:1–10		
20	Ephesians 3:14–15		
21	Ephesians 3:16–17		
22	Ephesians 3:18–19		
23	Ephesians 3:20–21		
24	Ephesians 3:14–21		
25	Philippians 2:2–3		
26	Philippians 2:4–6		
27	Philippians 2:7–8		
28	Philippians 2:9–11		
29	Philippians 2:1–11		
30	Psalm 1:1–2		
31	Psalm 1:3–4		
32	Psalm 1:5–6		
33	Psalm 1:1–6		
34	Matthew 22:36–38		
35	Matthew 22:39–40		

THE ETERNAL CHRIST

Most people in the world do not really understand who Jesus Christ is. Many think that He was a prophet, a very wise and good man sent from God. Others think He was the Son of God but came into existence when He was born in Bethlehem.

The truth is that Jesus was not simply a great man or prophet, nor did He have His "beginning" when He came as a little baby to be born in the manger at Bethlehem. It is true, as the books of Matthew and Luke tell us, that Jesus was born in Bethlehem; but God says that Jesus has always existed.

WHO IS JESUS CHRIST?

- As you look up each of the following verses, answer the questions below:

    1. Who created the heavens and Earth, according to Genesis 1:1? _____

    2. Who is the Word that was "in the beginning" with God and "was made flesh" to dwell among us? (John 1:1, 14) _____

    3. By whom were all things created according to John 1:3 and Hebrews 1:2?_____

    4. Read Genesis 1:26a and look carefully at the following: "And God (singular) said, Let us (plural) make man in our image, after our likeness." What is this verse telling you about who God is? _____

    _____

    _____

    _____

Explain how we were made in His image after His likeness.

_____

_____

_____

5.   First John 5:20 describes Jesus Christ in two ways. According to this verse, who is Jesus Christ? _____

6.   Explain the extent of the creation by Jesus Christ according to Colossians 1:16.

_____

_____

_____

_____

TWO IMPORTANT TRUTHS

•   For what reasons are the following concepts concerning Jesus extremely important for your life in regards to salvation and understanding who Jesus is?

1.   Genesis 1:1 and John 1:1 both use the phrases "in the beginning." What is important about this? _____

_____

2.   First John 5:20 says that Jesus is "eternal life." What is important about this?

_____

_____

"I AM"

It is very important to God that you understand the principle that Jesus Christ is truly God. God found several different ways to help you know the truth of this concept even though He knows your mind will not completely understand it. For further proof, God showed in different ways that Jesus is the one true God.

- Compare Exodus 3:14 with John 8:58. In each situation, who is talking, and what does He say about Himself?

  _____

  _____

  _____

- What do you think this term means, and what is important about its meaning?

  _____

  _____

  _____

  _____

Jesus is saying that, as God, He has no past or future. His life is not involved in the sphere of time as we know it. It is true that Jesus lived on the earth for approximately 33 years of time, but His life in eternity has no time limits whatsoever.

- Now look at John 8:59. What did the Jews try to do to Jesus because of what He said?

  _____

- Why do you think they did this?

  _____

  _____

To truly understand how this phrase helps us to understand that Jesus has always existed, look up the following two verses and find the part of the verse that explains more fully the phrase, "I am."

- Revelation 1:8 _____

  _____

- Revelation 1:17 _____

  _____

- How do these verses further support what has already been discussed concerning the person of Jesus Christ?

  _____

NAMES OF CHRIST

The Bible refers to Jesus in many different ways to show the many, many ways He meets our needs. Only a few of His many titles are given below. Look up each verse and write the term(s) given in each verse that explain who Jesus is.

Verse	Who Jesus Is
Psalm 118:22	
Isaiah 7:14	
Isaiah 9:6	
John 1:29	
John 6:32	
John 8:12	
John 10:11	
John 11:25	
Acts 3:14	
1 Corinthians 10:4	
1 Timothy 6:15	
Hebrews 4:14	
Hebrews 12:2	

MY RELATIONSHIP TO CHRIST

- Who do you say Jesus is? _____

- Is this important to you? _____ Why or why not? _____
  _____

- Based on the teacher's lesson, how can you "hear" God? _____
  _____
  _____
  _____

- Are you conscious of listening to the voice of God? _____

- In what ways do you hear His voice? _____
  _____

- Give an example of a time when He spoke to you in a specific way.
  _____
  _____
  _____

TEACHER'S LESSON NOTES

JESUS' PURPOSE ON EARTH

- " _____
  _____
  _____ " (1 John 4:14)

RESPONSES TO CHRIST

- Many did not _____ Him (John 1:10)

- Many did not _____ Him (John 1:11)

- Some did receive Him, and they were given _____ (John 1:12)

GOD WANTS TO _____ TO _____

- Through the _____ of _____

- By the _____ within the _____

- Through those placed as _____ in our _____

GOD WANTS _____ TO LISTEN TO _____

- We can _____ His _____

- We can _____ His _____

THE PROPHETIC CHRIST

The word *prophecy* in the Bible has two different meanings. One meaning refers to the proclaiming of the Word of God. A pastor or evangelist who teaches the Word of God and proclaims the need to repent from sin and live life for God is a prophet of God, for he is proclaiming and revealing the Word of God to others. The second meaning refers to the ability to foretell the future by inspiration from God. In this lesson, we will be discussing this second meaning.

There were literally hundreds of prophecies made about the life of Christ in the Old Testament that were fulfilled in the New Testament. Prophecies were made about the lineage or ancestry of Christ, about His birth, and particularly about His betrayal and death on the cross. Detail after detail was foretold about the life of Christ centuries before He walked on the earth.

The Old and New Testaments tell of the promise of God to all people. The Old Testament is a preparation for the coming of Jesus into the world. It prophesies (or foretells) what Christ would do on the earth. The New Testament begins with the birth of Christ and tells of the fulfillment of everything that was told (or prophesied) about Jesus in the Old Testament.

JESUS CHRIST IN PROPHECY

The prophecies of Christ generally fall into one of two categories: prophecies that describe a kingly Messiah and prophecies that show a suffering Savior. Most scholars of the Old Testament were awaiting the king who would rescue them from all their trials and earthly problems. So when Christ came to Earth and suffered on the cross, they did not recognize him as that same king. If they had focused on the entire Scriptures, they would have seen that Jesus, the suffering Savior, was also the kingly Messiah.

- Compare the Old Testament verse to the New Testament verse and explain what prophecy was fulfilled through Christ. Beside each prophecy, write a "K" If the prophecy describes Jesus as King or "S" if the prophecy describes the suffering Savior.

O. T. Verse	N. T. Verse	Prophecy Fulfilled	K/S
Psalm 22:18	Mark 15:24		
Psalm 34:20	John 19:33–36		
Psalm 41:9	Mark 14:10		
Psalm 68:18	Luke 24:51		
Psalm 69:21	John 19:29		
Psalm 110:1	Hebrews 10:12		
Psalm 110:4	Hebrews 6:20		
Isaiah 7:14	Matthew 1:18–23		
Isaiah 9:1–2	Matthew 4:12–16		
Isaiah 50:6	Matthew 27:30		
Isaiah 61:1	Matthew 3:16		
Jeremiah 31:15	Matthew 2:16–18		
Hosea 11:1	Matthew 2:14–15		
Micah 5:2	Matthew 2:1 Luke 2:4–6		
Zechariah 9:9	John 12:12–15		
Zechariah 11:12–13	Matthew 26:15		
Malachi 3:1	Matthew 11:7–10		

ISAIAH 53

Isaiah 53 was written completely with Jesus in mind. It would be impossible, except for the inspiration of the Holy Spirit, for the prophet Isaiah to have understood the sufferings of Jesus so completely and as accurately. The Lord knew what Jesus was to suffer and explained what would happen centuries before Jesus was born in Bethlehem.

Each verse has several descriptions of some aspect of what Christ did for us. For each verse, find one phrase and explain how it explicitly refers to Christ or our relationship to Christ.

Verse	Phrase	How It Refers to Christ
1		
2		
3		
4		
5		
6		
7		
8		
9		
10		
11		
12		

THE LAMB OF GOD

- When John the Baptist first saw Jesus, he referred to Him in a very interesting way. How did John the Baptist acknowledge Jesus in John 1:29? _____

    _____

    _____

Now look at the following verses and explain what they have to say about Jesus as the Passover Lamb and sacrifice for our sins.

- 1 Corinthians 5:7— _____

    _____

    _____

- 1 Peter: 1:19— _____

    _____

    _____

- Revelation 5:12— _____

    _____

    _____

Remember, the sacrificing and shedding of the blood of the lamb in the Old Testament did not take away the sins of the people. When they sacrificed a lamb, they were admitting to God that they could not rid themselves of their own sin but needed a Savior. They were trusting God to send Jesus Christ, the Lamb of God, to sacrifice Himself and shed His own blood for them.

MY RELATIONSHIP TO CHRIST

- I understand that the details of the life of Christ are given throughout the Old Testament. This is important to me because . . .

    _____

    _____

At the core of this lesson is recognizing the integrity of God. This quality is at the root of character strength. Integrity means honesty and truthfulness in every area of our lives. It means we can be trusted; it means that our words mean something; it means that we value who we are. God is truth. His promises have always been kept. We can always trust Him to mean what He says. He wants this part of His character to be an integral part of our lives.

- What promises or commitments do I have in my life right now?

  _____

  _____

- Why is it important to keep these promises or commitments?

  _____

  _____

TEACHER'S LESSON NOTES

DEFINITIONS:

- Testament: A _____ of _____

- Prophecy:

  - The _____ of the _____ of _____ (preaching)

  - The ability to _____ by _____ from _____

- Inspiration: God _____ and _____ people to _____ His message

- The _____ Testament continually says, "_____."

- The _____ Testament says, "Christ _____."

The Word of God Is the Story of Jesus Christ

THE PROMISE TO _____ AND _____

- A response of _____

- God made _____ of _____ (Gen. 3:21)

ABRAHAM IS WILLING TO _____ HIS _____

- A _____ of God's _____ of His only _____, _____

- "God will provide _____ a _____ for a burnt offering" (Gen. 22:8)

THE PASSOVER LAMB

- The _____ of the _____ was placed on the _____

- The _____ of the _____ saved the Israelite homes from death

THE BOOK OF _____

- The _____ must be a _____ male

- The _____ from the _____ must be sprinkled on the altar

THE BIRTH AND CHILDHOOD OF CHRIST

For centuries, God had used His Word and His creation to explain that the kingly Messiah and the suffering Savior would be born. Prophets and teachers had proclaimed the coming of the Messiah. Priests had made sacrifices, looking forward to the time when an animal sacrifice would no longer be necessary to symbolize atonement for sin. And now, for approximately 400 years, God had been silent. It was a time of quiet waiting. Then, suddenly, out of eternity, God's voice proclaimed the time had come.

- Galatians 4:4 explains it this way: " _____

_____

_____

_____. "

THE FIRST PROCLAMATIONS

Very few people have ever seen angels. God says that we may have seen an angel and not even have been aware of who it was we were meeting. Angels are sent by God to minister to us and protect us in ways that we are usually not even aware of.

But now, God sent angels to proclaim or announce the greatest event in history. The Son of God was to be born in order to be the final sacrifice for the sin of man. The fulfillment of the promise given to Adam and Eve and to all those who believed throughout the centuries was to come to pass.

- Find the following verses. Tell whom the angel visited, the purpose of the visit, and the response.

Verses	Who Was Visited?	The Purpose	The Response
Luke 1:5–22			
Matthew 1:18–25			
Luke 1:26–38			
Luke 2:8–17			

MARY, THE MOTHER OF JESUS

Consider what it would be like to be a teenage young woman who is preparing to marry. You have been raised in very humble surroundings and have been very sheltered. You know from the Scriptures that someday, the Messiah will come to the earth.

How did Mary's life show that she was willing to serve God? Reread the passage regarding Mary's visitation by the angel and then read her response in Luke 1:26–56.

- As you read, think about the character of Mary and list those qualities that showed her relationship with God, and how she fulfilled prophecy.

1. _____

2. _____

3. _____

4. _____

5. _____

THE BIRTH OF CHRIST

Read the details of the birth of Jesus carefully in Luke 2:1–39.

Joseph loved his wife, Mary, and he understood the great responsibility he had undertaken. He knew that the child she was carrying was the Christ. Joseph took good care of her and protected her. When it was time for the birth of the child, they had to make a long trip to Bethlehem.

- Why was such a trip necessary at this time? _____

  _____

  _____

- While they were in Bethlehem, Mary gave birth to Jesus. Where did the birth take place? _____

  _____

- Why was this necessary?_____

  _____

- How did she take care of the baby under such circumstances? _____

  _____

  _____

THE SHEPHERDS

- During the night, the angels announced the birth of Jesus to the shepherds, and they came to the stable to worship Him. What does God's choice of shepherds tell you about how He sees people?_____

  _____

  _____

- How did Mary respond to what was happening? _____
  _____
  _____

A TRIP TO JERUSALEM

- After a period of time, Mary and Joseph took Jesus to Jerusalem. What was the purpose of this? _____
  _____

SIMEON AND ANNA

- While they were in Jerusalem, two people recognized Jesus as the Savior. Who first responded to Jesus in this way? _____

- What had God promised him? _____
  _____

- How did he recognize the Son of God? _____
  _____

- Who was Anna? _____
  _____

- What did she do when she saw Jesus? _____
  _____

THE WISE MEN AND THE FLIGHT INTO EGYPT

After presenting Jesus to the Lord in Jerusalem, Mary and Joseph returned to Bethlehem. Some events began to take place that could have taken the life of Jesus, but God protected the child. It was not meant that Jesus would die as a child in secret—He was to live His life openly and share many principles before dying on the cross in view of everyone.

- To understand these events, read each section of Scripture given below and explain what takes place. All the verses are from Matthew chapter 2.

Verses	Who Was Involved?	What Took Place?
1–2		
3–6		
7–8		
9–11		
12		
13–15		
16–18		
19–23		

JOURNEYS OF JESUS IN HIS EARLY LIFE

- As another review of the events we have discussed, use the map in this lesson to trace the journeys of Mary, Joseph, and Jesus. Draw a line from place to place. Begin to learn the places that were important in the life of Jesus.

Verses	Where He Traveled/Lived	Purpose
Matthew 2:1		
Luke 2:22–38		
Matthew 2:13–14		
Matthew 2:19–23		
Luke 2:42–46		
Luke 2:51–52		

JESUS' JOURNEYS AS A CHILD

- Label the following using a map in your Bible if necessary:

  - Sea of Galilee
  - Dead Sea
  - Jordan River
  - Galilee
  - Samaria
  - Judea
  - Label the cities given above and trace the path showing Jesus' early life.

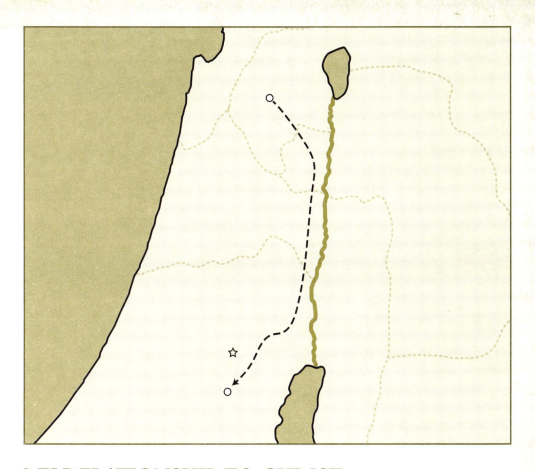

MY RELATIONSHIP TO CHRIST

- Review the story of the first few years of Jesus' life and explain in what ways God protected Jesus. _____

_____

_____

God had a great plan for Jesus. Jesus' life had a very definite purpose. It is important to understand that while the purpose of our lives can never be compared to the holy and awesome purpose of Jesus' death on the cross, our lives do have a unique purpose in God's plan. He is vitally concerned about our welfare and will protect us so that we can also fulfill our purpose. We must realize that just as Jesus and his family had problems and tribulations that even made them have to flee into Egypt for a while, still God was in control and protected them from harm. In our lives, we also will face problems, but God will be there to protect us through the problems.

- Think about your own life. Describe a time when you believe God was working to protect you in some way. _____

  _____

TEACHER'S LESSON NOTES

MATTHEW

- The _____ of _____

- _____ appears to _____

- The _____ of the _____

- The _____ into _____

MARK

Does not refer to the birth of Christ

LUKE

- _____ visits _____ and _____

- _____ about the _____ of _____

- The _____ of the _____

- Jesus is _____ to _____ in Jerusalem

- _____ and _____ recognize the _____

JOHN

"The Word was made flesh and dwelt among us." The Word, Jesus, is the Creator of all things.

JOHN THE BAPTIST, THE FORERUNNER OF CHRIST

The Bible tells us of only one incident in the life of Jesus when He was growing up. This was His visit with His parents to the temple at Jerusalem during Passover. It was during this visit that Jesus talked to the leaders in the temple and evidenced such great knowledge about God that He astonished all who heard Him.

- Other than this, we know only what is said of Him in Luke 2:51–52:

  _____

  _____

The time came, however, when Jesus was to begin his public ministry. This was when Jesus was approximately 30 years old. Just as God had used angels to proclaim His birth, God had planned a way to proclaim the ministry of His Son. The one who would announce Jesus was John the Baptist.

- Write a short paragraph reviewing the birth of John the Baptist. How was his birth announced? Who were his parents? What were his parents like? What was to be his purpose? (Luke 1:5–25; 57–80)

  _____

  _____

  _____

  _____

  _____

  _____

  _____

  _____

THE MINISTRY OF JOHN THE BAPTIST

John lived much of his life in the desert. When the timing was right, God called him to begin his special ministry.

- Describe how John the Baptist lived. (Matt. 3:4; Mark 1:6) _____

    _____

- Describe his ministry. (Matt. 3:1–3, 6, 11; Mark 1:2–4, 7–8; Luke 3:2–6)

    _____

    _____

    _____

    _____

- Who heard about John? How did they hear? How did they respond to his ministry? (Matt. 3:5; Mark 1:5; Luke 3:15) _____

    _____

    _____

    _____

    _____

- Who did many think John the Baptist was? How did he answer them? (John 1:19–27) _____

    _____

    _____

    _____

    _____

- How did John respond to the Sadducees and Pharisees? (Matt. 3:7–8)

    _____

    _____

- Describe his first meeting with Jesus. (Matt. 3:13–17)_____

    _____

    _____

    _____

    _____

THE DEATH OF JOHN THE BAPTIST

Read the following passages to learn what happened at the end of John the Baptist's life: Matthew 14:3–12 and Mark 6:17–30.

- Why was John imprisoned? _____

  _____

  _____

  _____

- What eventually happened to him? Why did Herod allow this to happen?

  _____

  _____

  _____

  _____

It is certainly sad to think of someone like John the Baptist dying as he did. And yet we must realize that as a Christian, God allows all things for a purpose. John had fulfilled God's purpose for his life. Yet, John the Baptist lost his life for having the courage to do what was right. But he has the eternal knowledge that he has done God's will.

- What did Christ say about John the Baptist in John 5:35? _____

  _____

  _____

- What did He mean by this? _____

  _____

THE CHARACTER OF JOHN THE BAPTIST

John the Baptist is one of the most interesting men in the Bible and an excellent example for your life. He was a man of outstanding courage who was proud to stand out from the crowd. The reason he was so strong was because he knew that God had a plan and purpose for his life that had been set forth from the beginning of time. You need to realize that though your name was not prophesied in the Bible, God knew all about you before you were born and has a special plan and purpose for your life too.

- Look up the verses to review John's life. Explain briefly what happened and then write one of the qualities below that show the character quality that was evident in that situation.

Obedience	Humility	Powerful preacher	Self-denial
Honored by Christ	Full of zeal	Holiness	Courage

Verse	What Happened	Character Quality
Matthew 3:4		
Matthew 3:7 Matthew 14:4		
Matthew 3:15		
Mark 1:5		
Mark 1:7 John 1:19–23		
Mark 6:20		
John 5:35		
Matthew 11:11 Luke 7:24–27		

MY RELATIONSHIP TO CHRIST

Now God does not want us to dress like John the Baptist dressed or eat the things he ate. But He does desire that we have the courage to stand for right and truth. As you think through this man's life and the purpose God had for him, consider how God can use the same character qualities in your life.

- How can you demonstrate each of the following characteristics?

  - Obedience _____
    _____

  - Self-denial _____
    _____

  - Humility _____
    _____

  - Full of zeal _____
    _____

  - Courage to stand for right _____
    _____

  - Holiness _____
    _____

TEACHER'S LESSON NOTES

JOHN THE BAPTIST IN THE SPOTLIGHT (JOHN 1:19–26)

Five Questions Asked of John

1. _____

2. _____

3. _____

4. _____

5. _____

Spiritual Condition of Jewish Leaders

- Spiritual _____

- Spiritual _____

- Spiritual _____

John Puts the Spotlight on Jesus (John 1:27–34)

- The _____ of John

- _____ lifted up

THE TEMPTATION OF CHRIST

Last week we studied about John the Baptist and how God used him to announce the beginning of Jesus' ministry on Earth. Just as John baptized Jesus, God spoke and said, "This is my beloved Son in whom l am well pleased."

- What happened to Jesus right after this took place according to Mark 1:11–12 and Matthew 3:17–4:1? _____

    _____

    _____

JESUS CAME TO DEFEAT SIN

- God had a purpose in leading Jesus to be tempted by Satan. Read 1 John 3:8 and write down four things this verse teaches.

    1. _____

        _____

    2. _____

        _____

    3. _____

        _____

    4. _____

        _____

Jesus' temptation showed the reason He came to Earth—to defeat sin.

Satan's History

- Before we can truly become victorious over the attacks of Satan, we must learn who he is. First of all, it is important to realize that, unlike God, Satan is a created being. Because all things were created by God except God Himself, who created Satan? (Review John 1:1–3.) _____

- God created Satan to be a beautiful creature who easily won the admiration of others. Study Isaiah 14:12–15 to see why he became the enemy of all humans.

    1. What was his original name, and where did he live at first? _____
    _____

    2. Where did the change begin in Satan? _____

    3. Satan began to use statements beginning with the words "l will . . ." five different times. List the five statements below:

        - I will _____

        - I will _____

        - I will _____

        - I will _____

        - I will _____

            - What does this continual use of the phrase "l will" tell you about the heart change of Satan? _____
            _____

            - Now read the last "l will" statement of Satan. Explain his overall attitude in your own words. _____
            _____
            _____
            _____

    4. What eventually will happen to Satan? _____
    _____

Satan's Names and Purpose

As a result of his pride and arrogance, Satan was cast out of heaven and eventually became a strong, controlling influence on the earth.

- Look up each verse indicated and write the phrase that explains what Satan is called. Then, in your own words, explain the earthly activities or purposes that he is responsible for based on the meaning of the Scripture.

Verses	What He Is Called	His Earthly Activities and Purpose
2 Corinthians 4:4		
2 Corinthians 11:14–15		
Ephesians 2:2		
Ephesians 6:12		
1 Peter 5:8		
Revelation 12:9		

JESUS IS TEMPTED BY SATAN

It is also important to realize that when Jesus was on Earth, He felt all the things we feel, and this included the pressure of facing temptation.

- Copy Hebrews 4:15 to see this even more clearly. _____
_____
_____
_____
_____

- Why do you think it was important for God to allow Jesus to be tempted as we are?

  _____

  _____

- According to Hebrews 4:15, Jesus was tempted just as we are tempted. These temptations come in three ways. List these three ways based on 1 John 2:16.

  1. _____

  2. _____

  3. _____

- Now when Satan came to Jesus in the wilderness, he first came when Jesus was at His weakest. In what way was Jesus weakened? (Luke 4:2) _____

  _____

This is the area in which Satan attacked Jesus first—the lust of the flesh. When this did not work, he tempted Him in the other two areas.

- On the following chart, explain the temptation that came from Satan and then explain Jesus' answer.

Area Attacked	Satan's Temptation	Jesus' Answer
Lust of the flesh Luke 4:3–4		
Lust of the eyes Luke 4:5–8		
Pride of life Luke 4:9–12		

- In each situation, what did Jesus use to defeat Satan? _____

- Now read Luke 4:13 carefully. What happened to Satan now, and what must we realize when we have resisted Satan? _____

  _____

Satan will never be as powerful as the Creator, because he received all his powers from God Himself. God has control over Satan and will ensure his defeat when Satan is cast into the lake of fire.

- We also have the power of God within us—the Holy Spirit. What does this tell you about your ability to use this power to resist Satan's attacks on your life?

  _____

  _____

  _____

MY RELATIONSHIP TO CHRIST

Satan is very smart. He finds our areas of weakness and tempts us there. For some, Satan might tempt them to steal; others may be tempted to get angry or fight; others may never steal or fight but may be tempted to cheat to get a good grade. Therefore we need to be aware of our weaknesses in order to guard against the attacks of Satan.

- Think of each of the three areas that we have discussed in this lesson and consider areas of weakness that may be used by Satan to tempt you.

  - Lust of the flesh _____

    _____

    _____

  - Lust of the eyes _____

    _____

    _____

  - Pride of life _____

    _____

    _____

TEACHER'S LESSON NOTES

GOD DOES NOT _____ US TO DO _____ (JAMES 1:13–15)

We are tempted by _____

We are tempted by _____

PRINCIPLES FROM 1 CORINTHIANS 10:12–13

We can easily _____ into _____

Every temptation is _____ to _____

God will not _____ temptation that you are _____ to _____

God will _____ a way of _____

    _____ to God

    _____ the Devil

    The result: _____

THREE IMPORTANT FIRSTS

After being baptized by John and confronting the devil in the wilderness, Jesus began his earthly ministry. His first year of ministry has often been called the year of inauguration. This means a year of beginnings. In this lesson we will discuss three events that happened during the beginning of the year of inauguration: the first disciples were called, the first miracle took place, and the first Passover during Christ's ministry took place.

THE FIRST DISCIPLES

Most people know that Jesus had twelve disciples. But most people think that they all became disciples at the same time. Actually, at first only five disciples were called. We will study about how they were chosen in John 1:35–51.

Andrew is one of the first two disciples mentioned in the beginning of verse 37. We find his name later in verse 40. The name of the other disciple isn't mentioned, but it was probably John, the writer of the one of the Gospels.

Verses	Disciple	Jesus' Question or Remarks	The Responses of the Disciples
37–39			
40–42			

43–45			
46–50			

THE FIRST MIRACLE

Jesus is known to have performed many miracles throughout His earthly ministry. The very first miracle took place in the town of Cana, which was about an hour's journey from Nazareth. Cana was a small, insignificant town very similar to Nazareth. Its inhabitants were humble, common people who were probably not known outside their village.

*   Why do you think Jesus chose this setting to perform His first miracle? _____

    _____

*   Now read the details of the miracle in John 2:1–11. Write a paragraph explaining what took place. Include details that you notice concerning Jesus' relationship to His mother, how well known Jesus was at this time, and the obvious power that He had.

    _____

    _____

    _____

    _____

    _____

    _____

*   According to John 2:12, where did Jesus go from Cana and who was traveling with Him? _____

    _____

THE FIRST PASSOVER

Christ commemorated four Passovers during His earthly ministry. Obviously, this is not the first Passover, for it took place in Egypt centuries before Christ was born. This is the first Passover of Christ's ministry on Earth.

John 2:13 tells us that Jesus traveled to Jerusalem. The purpose of this visit to the holy city was to be there at the time of the Passover celebration.

Read the story of what took place there in John 2:13–25 and answer the following questions.

1. What did Jesus find taking place in the temple? _____
   _____
   _____

2. What did He do in response to what He found? _____
   _____
   _____

3. There were Jews standing by watching what Jesus did. They approached Him and questioned Him about His actions. What was confusing to them about the analogy that Christ was making? _____
   _____
   _____
   _____
   _____

4. Three years later, the disciples would remember what Jesus had said to the Jews at this time. What specifically did they remember that helped them to believe?
   _____
   _____
   _____

5. Jesus stayed in Jerusalem after this for the feast of the Passover. He did other miracles during this time. What effect did this have on the people?
   _____

Christ's actions in regard to the moneychangers and merchants in the temple showed several things about His personality and character. Using phrases from the story or your own ideas based on the story, explain what you learned about Christ the following areas:

- His Boldness and Strength _____

_____

_____

- His Holiness _____

_____

_____

- His Wrath _____

_____

_____

- His Authority as God _____

_____

_____

MY RELATIONSHIP TO CHRIST

Jesus referred to the temple as His own body, which would be raised after three days. There is another important analogy to be made concerning the temple and the sin that was taking place within the temple.

- Read 1 Corinthians 3:16–17 and 1 Corinthians 6:19–20 and explain this analogy. After your explanation, discuss what God would do if He cleansed your temple in the same way Jesus cleansed the temple in Jerusalem. _____

_____

_____

_____

_____

- What work would He have to do? _____

_____

TEACHER'S LESSON NOTES

THE WEDDING AT CANA—SYMBOLS OF CHRIST

The Time of the Event

- The _____ Day

  - The _____

  - The _____

The Problem

- The Waterpots

  - _____ waterpots

  - The waterpots were _____

  - The waterpots were made of _____

- The _____ Was Gone

The Solution

- The _____ responsibility

- The _____ power

The Results

- _____ was produced

- _____ was glorified

NICODEMUS FINDS JESUS

Jesus stayed in Jerusalem after He cleansed the temple of the merchants and moneychangers. The time of year was during the spring of the year 27 A. D. The Bible does not say where the meeting with Nicodemus took place, but it was a quiet place where two people could talk privately. Jesus had probably gone off by Himself to pray and think about the events that had been happening. Perhaps Nicodemus found Jesus in one of the gardens around the city. Since it was spring, the evening air was warm when Nicodemus approached.

THE MEETING WITH NICODEMUS

- To learn more about Nicodemus, read John 3:1–2 and list as many points about him that you can find. Include facts that indicate what Nicodemus thought about Jesus.

  1. _____

  2. _____

  3. _____

  4. _____

  5. _____

- How do you think Nicodemus knew so much about Jesus? _____

  _____

  _____

- How did his actions show both cowardice and courage? _____

  _____

  _____

  _____

THE NEW BIRTH

Nicodemus and Jesus talked about very important ideas that were obviously new to Nicodemus. We can be assured that Jesus saw right into Nicodemus's heart and began to answer his heart's need before Nicodemus even asked a question. Most probably, Nicodemus did not even know what to ask.

- What did Jesus tell Nicodemus right away? (John 3:3) _____

_____

_____

- How did Nicodemus respond, and how did Jesus explain what He meant? (John 3:4–9) _____

_____

_____

_____

Explain the ideas that Jesus taught Nicodemus in the following passages:

- John 3:9–12 _____

_____

_____

_____

- John 3:13–16 _____

_____

_____

_____

- John 3:17–18 _____

_____

_____

_____

- John 3:19–21 _____

_____

_____

_____

- This message of the new birth was the first teaching of Christ's ministry on Earth. Why do you think that this was His first subject to speak about?

_____

_____

THE PHYSICAL BIRTH AND SPIRITUAL BIRTH

It is no accident that Jesus refers to salvation as a birth of the Spirit. To understand the analogy more completely, we will look at different aspects of our physical birth and compare them to what happens when we are born of God. Explain how each of the following facts corresponds in some way to your spiritual birth.

Physical Birth	Spiritual Birth
A blood relationship	
Begins our relationship with an earthly father	
The relationship with the father lasts forever.	
God gives life to the child.	
The child is given a name.	
The child is given milk until he can eat meat.	
The birth of the child brings great joy.	
The child is given a new home.	
The parents are responsible to meet the needs of the child.	

JESUS CAME TO SAVE THE LOST

- The most important reason that Jesus came to the earth was to save those who are lost. Later on, Jesus shared two short parables or stories to teach this important point. Turn to Luke 15:1–10 and give a summary of each parable below.

    - First Parable: _____

      _____

      _____

      _____

    - Second Parable: _____

      _____

      _____

      _____

- What is the theme of the two parables? _____

    _____

    _____

    _____

- Who was listening to the parables that needed to understand that they were "lost" so that they could be "saved"? _____

MY RELATIONSHIP TO CHRIST

The key idea of this lesson is the message that Jesus had for Nicodemus and for you: "Ye must be born again."

- What does this mean, and how does it apply to your life? _____

    _____

    _____

TEACHER'S LESSON NOTES:

WHAT IS THE NEW LIFE?

- It is _____

- It is a _____

- It brings no _____

- It is a life of _____

- It is a _____ of _____

HOW DO YOU RECEIVE THIS LIFE?

- Recognize that you _____

- Recognize that _____ your sin to
  _____

- Repent _____

- Believe that _____ is the _____ of God who
  _____ to pay the _____

- Believe that you have _____ through _____

JUDEA, SAMARIA, GALILEE

JESUS' FIRST YEAR OF MINISTRY

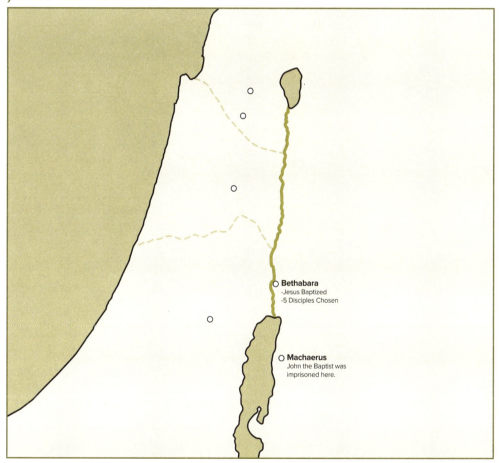

- Label the following: Sea of Galilee, Dead Sea, Jordan River, Judea, Samaria, and Galilee. Then label and follow the places Jesus traveled during His first year of ministry as the lesson instructs you to do.

THE YEAR OF INAUGURATION

- During Jesus' first year of ministry, we have seen that He traveled through all three provinces. Using the map, follow the journey of Jesus during this first year to understand exactly where He traveled. Beside each place on the map, write the name of the place. Then explain below what happened at that place.

  1. Bethabara (when He first went there from Nazareth) _____

  _____

  2. The wilderness of Judea _____

  _____

  3. Bethabara (when He went there after leaving the Judean wilderness)

  _____

  4. Cana _____

  _____

  5. Jerusalem _____

  _____

THE MINISTRY IN SAMARIA

- Now during the time of the Passover and the meeting with Nicodemus, Jesus was preparing to go back to Galilee. To return to Galilee, He would travel through Samaria. Read John 3:22–36. Who had preceded Jesus in the Samaritan villages? (Aenon near Salim is in Samaria, close to the city of Sychar.) What was he saying and doing there? How must this have prepared the Samaritans for Jesus' visit?

  _____

  _____

  _____

  _____

  _____

- When Jesus left Judea for Galilee, what probably caused Him to leave when He did? Read the following verses in the order given to learn what had happened: Luke

3:19–20, Matthew 4:12, and John 4:1–4. _____

_____ _____

_____

_____

_____

- Do you think Jesus was afraid? _____

- Then why do you think He left at this time? _____

_____

THE WOMAN AT THE WELL

- John 4:4–6. Where did this take place? Be specific. _____

_____

- John 4:7–9. What did Jesus ask the woman, and why did this surprise her?

_____

_____

_____

- John 4:10–15. What did the water symbolize? _____

_____

_____

- John 4:16–19. How does this passage show the omniscience of Christ?

_____

_____

_____

- John 4:20–26. What did Jesus teach the woman? _____

_____

- John 4:31–34. What was the difference in the meaning of the word *meat*?

_____

_____

_____

- John 4:35–38. What lesson about evangelism did Christ teach the disciples?

  _____

  _____

- John 4:27–30 and 39–42. What resulted from the talk with the woman?

  _____

  _____

Compare the meeting with Nicodemus with the woman at the well. Note the ideas under Nicodemus and explain the difference to be noted.

Nicodemus	Woman at the Well
a man	
Jew	
very religious	
ranked high in society	
lived a moral, righteous life	
sought out Christ	
brought no one else to Christ	

It is important to realize that though these two people were completely different in every way, Christ loved them both and took the necessary time to show them the true way of salvation.

THE HEALING OF THE NOBLEMAN'S SON

- Read the story of Jesus' second miracle in John 4:46–54 and answer the following questions.

  1. Where did this take place? _____

     _____

  2. What type of person do you think the nobleman was? _____

     _____

  3. What was the problem? _____

4. How was the boy healed? Be specific. _____

_____

_____

5. What was the result of this miracle? _____

_____

MORE MAP WORK

- Now add the following to the map and explain what happened at each place.

    1. Sychar _____

    _____

    2. Cana in Galilee _____

    _____

    3. Nazareth (Luke 4:16–21) _____

    _____

- Note the place called Machaerus where John the Baptist was imprisoned.

MY RELATIONSHIP TO CHRIST

In our lesson this week, we saw two times that Jesus left a place due to His great popularity and because of great rejection. Jesus is in control of His destiny. What others think of Him or how they treat Him has nothing to do with Jesus' actions or attitudes. He is set on His purpose for His life; He knows how He will act, and nothing will move Him from the path He knows to be right.

Jesus provides you that same type of control. It is difficult not to feel hurt and sad when you are rejected, and it is equally difficult not to feel "puffed up" when you are very popular. What others think therefore should have no effect on you because the feelings and attitudes of others can change from moment to moment. You need to be able to stand for right no matter what others think.

- Be honest! How do rejection and popularity affect you?

_____

_____

- What things will you do or not do regardless of other people's responses?

  _____

  _____

TEACHER'S LESSON NOTES

JESUS RETURNS TO NAZARETH (LUKE 4:16–30)

The Purposes of His Ministry

- To _____ the _____ to the _____

- To _____ the _____

- To _____

- To _____ of _____ to the _____

- To set at _____ the _____

- To _____ the _____ of the Lord

He _____ Who He Is

He Is _____

Jesus Is Not Swayed from His Calling

- By _____

- By _____

JESUS ORDAINS HIS DISCIPLES

We are now entering the second year of Christ's ministry on Earth. He has been baptized by John the Baptist, performed two miracles, chosen disciples, and attended the Passover in Jerusalem, where He cleansed the temple of moneychangers and merchants. But already His fame has spread over the land. Now as his second year begins, you will see that He becomes very popular with the masses of people. Thousands will follow Him to listen to His words and to be healed of infirmities. This will be the year of popularity. But as this year develops, you will also notice that small groups will begin to talk against Him and will want His ministry to come to an end.

FOUR DISCIPLES CALLED

During Jesus' first year of earthly ministry, we saw that five disciples had been chosen. At this point, they still worked at their occupations and lived with their families. Now Jesus was ready to choose His remaining disciples and call all of them to come apart and follow Him completely.

- Read Luke 5:1–11 to see how this began to happen. You will see in verse 3 that Jesus entered Simon Peter's fishing boat to speak. Why was this? _____ _____ _____

- After He had finished speaking, He told Simon Peter to do something. What problem had Peter had, and what did Jesus tell him to do? _____ _____ _____ _____

- What two results do we see happening from this? (vv. 7–8) _____
  _____
  _____
  _____

- Peter immediately left his work to follow Jesus. . Read Matthew 4:18–22. Who also left their fishing to begin to follow Jesus at this time? _____

- What did Jesus promise them they would do? _____
  _____

MATTHEW IS CHOSEN

- Most of the disciples that Jesus chose were fishermen. Now Jesus goes into the city and picks someone who is very disliked in the community. (See Luke 5:27–32 and Mark 2:13–17.)

  1. What did Levi (Matthew) do for a living? _____

  2. Where did Levi invite Jesus to come, and who was there? _____
     _____

  3. Who was upset at this, and why were they upset? _____
     _____
     _____

  4. How did Jesus respond to their accusations? _____
     _____
     _____

THE TWELVE ARE ORDAINED

Some of the names of the twelve apostles you recognize immediately, while others are not so familiar because they are not often mentioned. Most of the disciples seem to play a minor role in Jesus' ministry, but this is not true. Jesus had a great plan and purpose for each of them that was completed after His death.

All of the disciples came from Galilee except Judas, who came from Judea. They were all different in their personalities and abilities, and Jesus wanted to use each of them in a particular way. Perhaps Jesus chose these men to be a typical group, a sample of what the Church was to be, including not only those who had special talents for leadership but also those who had less obvious abilities. They walked with Him, learned from Him, failed, and grew stronger and stronger. They would be ready to carry the gospel after Christ had ascended to heaven to be with His Father.

- From what you have read, what types of men did Jesus choose to be His first disciples, and how do they represent all people? _____

  _____

- List the first five disciples that Jesus called. Refer to Lesson 6 to find their names if necessary. Finally, turn to Luke 6:13–16 and Mark 3:13–19 and complete the list of the twelve disciples Jesus had chosen.

  1. _____

  2. _____

  3. _____

  4. _____

  5. _____

  6. _____

  7. _____

  8. _____

  9. _____

  10. _____

  11. _____

  12. _____

- Jesus called these men to a specific purpose that He outlined for them. Using Mark 1:17 and 3:14–15, list the five purposes He had for His apostles.

    1. _____

    2. _____

    3. _____

    4. _____

    5. _____

- Jesus did not choose His disciples without a great deal of prayer. Explain the circumstances in which Jesus chose His disciples from Luke 6:12–13.

    _____

    _____

    _____

CONDITIONS OF DISCIPLESHIP

- We are all called to be disciples. Jesus explained several qualifications for those who would follow Him. Look up each verse below and explain in your own words what you think Jesus asked of the twelve disciples and is asking of us as well.

    - Matthew 16:24 _____

        _____

    - Luke 14:26 _____

        _____

    - Luke 14:33 _____

        _____

    - John 8:31 _____

        _____

    - John 15:8 _____

        _____

SECRET DISCIPLESHIP

As the works of Jesus became known, many hundreds of people began to follow Him openly as did the twelve. But there were some who believed in their hearts that this was the Messiah but would not publicly show their belief in Jesus. As you look up the verses, find out who was secret in their belief and why they were secretive.

Verse	Who Was Secretive?	Why Were They Secretive?
John 3:1–2		
John 12:42		
John 19:38		

- Look up Proverbs 29:25 and explain why people hide their faith in Jesus and why we should feel free to proclaim Him publicly. _____
_____
_____
_____

MY RELATIONSHIP TO CHRIST

It is easy to be open about our faith in Jesus when we are with our Christian friends or with our family. But many times we have difficulty being open about our faith in Jesus Christ. We fear what others will think of us instead of being proud of what we have and being willing to stand for the truth. Sometimes, this fear even shows up when we are asked what school we attend.

- Can you think of instances when fear took hold of you and you did not stand for Christ? _____
_____
_____

- How can you overcome this type of fear the next time such a situation comes?

  _____

  _____

- Now tell of a time when you were able to boldly and proudly proclaim your faith and trust in Jesus. _____

  _____

  _____

TEACHER'S LESSON NOTES

THE TRAINING OF THE DISCIPLES

They Were _____ Jesus

They _____ from Jesus

- By _____ His _____

- By _____ to His _____

- By _____

THE YEAR OF POPULARITY

From the very beginning of His ministry, the gospels tell of Jesus' mighty works. As we read about each of the miracles, we see Jesus' genuine love for people. His primary concern was always to use His power to help the people out of genuine love and concern for them as individuals. These mighty works also gave evidence that God was present. Nothing attracted more attention than the miracles. The news of the miracles spread like wildfire through every town and village. Wherever Jesus went, the streets were soon lined with those who had need of healing and those who were just curious. Read Matthew 4:23–25 and discuss the extent of Jesus' fame at this time.

_____

_____

_____

_____

_____

_____

_____

THE PEOPLE LOVED AND FOLLOWED JESUS

As you read each of the following accounts, note how the people continually responded to Jesus. First explain the miracles that took place and then discuss the response of the people.

Verses	What Jesus Did	How the People Responded
Mark 1:21–28 Luke 4:31–37		

Mark 1:29–33		
Mark 1:39–45		
Mark 2:1–12		

THE PHARISEES BEGIN TO MURMUR

* Reread Mark 2:1–12. What were the scribes beginning to think among themselves?

  _____

  _____

  _____

* How did Jesus respond to their questions? _____

  _____

  _____

  _____

THE SABBATH DAY

Two important situations happened on the Sabbath day, which began to stir up the scribes and Pharisees even more. According to Jewish law, the Sabbath was on Saturday, the last day of the week. It was to be a holy day, set aside only for God. No one was to do work of any kind on the Sabbath. The Jews even cooked their food on Friday so they would not have to prepare anything on the Sabbath.

* With this in mind, read Mark 2:23–28 and Luke 6:1–5 and discuss the following.

1. What were the disciples doing? _____

_____

_____

2. Why were the Pharisees upset at this? _____

_____

_____

3. What example did Jesus use to rebuke them? _____

_____

_____

_____

4. What two points did Jesus make in Mark 2:27–28? _____

_____

_____

_____

• On another Sabbath day shortly thereafter, Jesus entered a synagogue and began teaching. In the synagogue was a man with a withered hand. Read Luke 6:6–7 and explain the attitude of the Pharisees and scribes at this point._____

_____

_____

_____

_____

_____

• Now read the passages from Mark 3:1–6 and Luke 6:6–11 and answer the following.

1. What did Jesus cause to happen to the man with the withered hand? _____

_____

_____

2. How did the Pharisees respond? _____

_____

_____

3. What lesson was Jesus trying to teach them? _____

_____

_____

THE POOL OF BETHESDA

About this time the feast of the Passover was again to take place in Jerusalem. Jesus and his disciples went again to the Passover celebration. As they went through one of the gates, the sheep gate, into the city, they came to the pool of Bethesda where many sick people were lying. As Jesus approached, He noticed one man in particular.

*   Describe the man and what happened to him as specifically as you can as you read John 5:1–9. _____

_____

_____

_____

_____

The pool of water, cut from a solid rock, is filled by rain. It is about 55 feet in length and 12 feet wide. It is approached by a flight of steps that wind steeply down to the water.

*   How does this fact enter into the story of John 5? _____

_____

_____

Again, the Jewish religious leaders took note of what had happened. They approached the man who had just been healed and began to rebuke him. What did they say to him, and how did he respond?

Verses	What Was Said?	What Was the Response?
10–11		

12–15		

- Once again, what response came from the religious leaders regarding Jesus? (vs. 16)

  _____

  _____

- For what two reasons were they so angered at Him according to verse 18?

  1. _____

     _____

  2. _____

     _____

MY RELATIONSHIP TO CHRIST

We have pointed out the fact in this lesson that Jesus healed people to prove He was the Christ. Obviously this is true; but if that is all we understand about His miracles, then we miss the true meaning of who Jesus is. Jesus healed people because He loved them. Jesus loved the man with the withered hand. He loved the man who had been paralyzed for so many, many years.

The Pharisees loved laws that would not bend. To them, laws and rules were more important than people. The recognition of the Sabbath laws was far more important to them than the people Jesus healed.

And it is true that Jesus could have healed the same people on another day. But He chose the Sabbath to teach this very important lesson. Since it was such an important question for Jesus to raise, you need to ask yourself the same questions. How important are people to you? Are you more interested in helping someone than in guarding your own reputation? Are you willing to befriend someone who needs a friend at the risk of losing other friends?

TEACHER'S LESSON NOTES

THE POOL OF BETHESDA

The Man Who Needed Healing

- _____

- _____

- _____

- _____

- _____

The Healer

- _____

- Did not need _____ to _____

- _____

THE SERMON ON THE MOUNT (PART 1)

In our last lesson, we began to see a definite difference in priorities between the attitudes of the Pharisees, scribes, and other Jewish religious leaders and the attitudes of Jesus.

- The Pharisees were concerned with _____
  _____

- Jesus focused on _____
  _____

Next, Jesus delivered His greatest sermon, which we call the Sermon on the Mount. In it, Jesus explained in even more detail what His ministry meant. He explained that duty to external laws, rules, and observances is not as important as the inner spirit, or attitude, of one's conduct. Jesus knew that when the heart is right, the details will take care of themselves. We should not obey rules out of duty but out of desire.

Jesus never emphasized rules or laws. Rather, He taught us principles by which to live.

- A rule tells us _____

- A principle shows us _____
  _____

Jesus taught that all day long the thoughts that occupy your mind and heart (your own "secret place") determine your actions. What you are on the inside is what you will be outwardly. But how you act will not change your heart or make you acceptable to God. It's dangerous simply to do what Christians are expected to do, instead of having a right attitude or motive for obeying God. This is how the Pharisees acted.

The Sermon on the Mount opens with the eight Beatitudes—eight principles—that apply to our everyday lives. They are eight mental attitudes that we need to have. If these attitudes are kept inside our hearts, everything else will be right; if these attitudes are wrong, nothing else can be right. Jesus does not give us detailed instructions on what to do or not to do, but rather shows us how to think and feel and be.

THE BEATITUDES

To help you understand the meaning of the word "beatitude," think of it as an "attitude to have". As your teacher discusses each Beatitude, take notes on the important ideas so you will understand the principles of life that Jesus is teaching you.

1. "Blessed are the poor in spirit: for theirs is the kingdom of heaven" (Matt. 5:3).
   _____
   _____

2. "Blessed are they that mourn: for they shall be comforted" (Matt. 5:4).
   _____
   _____

3. "Blessed are the meek: for they shall inherit the earth" (Matt. 5:5).
   _____
   _____

4. "Blessed are they which do hunger and thirst after righteousness: for they shall be filled" (Matt. 5:6). _____
   _____
   _____

5. "Blessed are the merciful: for they shall obtain mercy" (Matt. 5:7).
   _____
   _____

6. "Blessed are the pure in heart: for they shall see God" (Matt. 5:6).
   _____
   _____

7. "Blessed are the peacemakers: for they shall be called the children of God" (Matt. 5:9).

_____

_____

8. "Blessed are they which are persecuted for righteousness" sake: for theirs is the kingdom of heaven. Blessed are ye, when men shall revile you, and persecute you, and shall say all manner of evil against you falsely, for my sake. Rejoice, and be exceeding glad: for great is your reward in heaven: for so persecuted they the prophets which were before you" (Matt. 5:10–12).

_____

_____

THE RICH YOUNG MAN

One of the saddest passages in the Scriptures is the story of the rich young man who missed one of the great opportunities of life and "went away sorrowful, for he had great possessions" (Matt. 19:22). The rich young man is a picture or symbol of all of us. Most people are not rich in money, but their possessions and personal ideas and attitudes are so important to them that they trust those things instead of Christ.

Read the story of the rich young man in Luke 18:18–30 and answer the following questions based on your understanding of the Beatitudes.

- What question did he ask Jesus? _____

  _____

- What kind of life did the young man lead? _____

- How do you know? _____

  _____

  _____

  _____

- In discussing these things, was Jesus focusing on the external or internal values of life? _____

- What did Jesus ask him to do that focused on the inner character and values of life?

  _____

  _____

- What did Jesus mean by this? _____

  _____

  _____

- Then, in talking with His disciples about the things that are truly important in life, He explained Himself further. Read Luke 18:28–30 and explain what Jesus meant based on your study of the Beatitudes. _____

  _____

  _____

  _____

AS A MAN THINKS . . .

The Beatitudes have definitely emphasized that our outward actions begin in our minds. What we think becomes what we do. Read Matthew 5:13–16 and explain the two analogies that Jesus used to explain this truth.

1. _____

2. _____

In the remainder of Matthew 5, Jesus relates several types of life situations in which those such as the Pharisees focus on the external while He helps us to understand that inner attitudes and values are even more important.

Passage	External Law	Internal Attitude
Matt. 5:21–24		

What should you do to be truly right with God in this situation? Go to the person and be reconciled to the person before worshipping God.

Passage	External Law	Internal Attitude
Matt. 5:27–28		

MY RELATIONSHIP TO CHRIST

- Explain the difference between the law (rules) and principles. _____
  _____
  _____

- Give an example of a rule and then of the principle behind the rule that has helped you in your life. _____
  _____
  _____

- Why is this particular principle important to you? _____
  _____
  _____

TEACHER'S LESSON NOTES

Beatitudes (Matt. 5:3–12)	Lord's Prayer (Matt. 6:9–13)
"Blessed are the poor in spirit."	
"Blessed are they that mourn." "Blessed are the meek."	
"Blessed are they which do hunger and thirst after righteousness."	

"Blessed are the merciful."	
"Blessed are the pure in heart."	
"Blessed are they which are persecuted for righteousness' sake."	
"Blessed are the peacemakers."	

THE SERMON ON THE MOUNT (PART 2)

Many years ago, God had given the law to Israel through Moses. As the Israelites tried to follow the terms of the law, there grew up around it many traditions and regulations that were not given by God. Many people found themselves doing many things to try to obey the law while forgetting who God was. God, the giver of the law, was being lost in a multitude of traditions that had no meaning. A person was accused of plowing if he happened to drag a stick on the Sabbath, and another was accused of reaping if he pulled a single hair from his head. A person could not carry water to an ox on the Sabbath day, but he could lead the ox to water. Such ridiculousness did not lead people to know God.

Jesus saw the people wandering aimlessly around as sheep without a shepherd. He came to help these people—not to add to their burdens of life. Jesus did not deny that breaking the law was sin, but he went a step further and showed how sin had something to do with what goes on inside a person. The Beatitudes that we studied in Lesson 11 point us to our inner motives and attitudes rather than focusing only on external actions. Jesus wanted to teach that sin lay in our mind and spirit.

This lesson completes the Sermon on the Mount. As you study the lessons taught in this great sermon, recognize that Jesus is continually pointing to the heart and motives of man.

RESIST NOT EVIL

It is very natural for any of us to outwardly resist any undesirable circumstance in our lives. We do not ever wish to deal with unpleasantness, especially if it is something that is against us or hurtful to us in any way. And yet life is filled with both good and bad. Life is filled with both joy and sorrow. God wants us to learn that if we resist the bad or unwanted circumstances, we give it more power over us. This happens because it becomes important and bigger in our minds than it is in reality. Think about some of the things you have worried about. If you are honest, most of these things did not even happen. You worried and made them more important than they really were. That is why God says "resist not evil" (Matt. 5:39). Instead, turn your attention to God and allow Him to deal with the problem for you.

As you study the following passages, compare what it is natural to do and what Jesus is teaching us to do instead. Again, Jesus is focusing on our inward attitudes rather than our outward actions.

Passage	Natural Action	Spiritual Attitude
Matt. 5:38–39		
Matt. 5:40–42		
Matt. 5:43–44		

- In verses 45 through 47, Jesus gives three examples concerning our attitude towards those who hurt us. List the three examples below.

1. _____
   _____

2. _____
   _____

3. _____
   _____

Just as we need to learn to focus on our heart attitudes and motives regarding what we do, so should we focus on an internal relationship with God before we worry about material goods of value that we might accumulate. It is not that things are wrong or bad, but when our primary concern is on things rather than on our internal character, our life is out of focus. If you are putting God first in your life, you will find that you will enjoy the external things of life better also.

Passage	What We Should Do	How We Should Do It
Matt. 5:16		
Matt. 6:1–4		
Matt. 6:5–8		

- Now state the general principle concerning all of these things in your own words. Base your ideas on Matthew 6:19–21. _____

_____

_____

_____

_____

_____

_____

GIVE AND IT SHALL BE GIVEN UNTO YOU

This principle is basically the concept of sowing and reaping. God wants us to learn that as we think, speak, and act toward others, so will others think, speak, and act toward us. Whatever sort of conduct we give out, we are inevitably going to get back. The good that we do to others we shall receive back, and the evil that we do to others we shall receive back, too. This does not mean that the same people whom we treat well or badly will be the actual ones to return the action. Sometimes that does happen. But more importantly, someone else who knows nothing whatever of the previous actions will, nevertheless, repay them. If we truly understood this principle of life, it would change our life completely.

- As you read each of the portions of Scripture below, write a life principle in your own words based on the Scripture.

  - Matthew 7:1–2 _____
  _____
  _____

  - Mathew 7:3–5 _____
  _____
  _____

  - Matthew 7:7–8 _____
  _____
  _____

  - Matthew 7:9–11 _____
  _____
  _____

  - Matthew 7:13–14 _____
  _____
  _____

BY THEIR FRUITS

Truth is just as essential a part of the Christian message as is love. God is love, and God is also truth. Unless these two qualities are balanced in our lives, we do not get wisdom; for wisdom is the perfect balance of truth and love. A spoiled child may receive much love, for example, but not enough truth. An abused child may receive much truth but little love. Either type of training is cruel; for each way is out of balance, and the child suffers.

In wisdom there is a balance between showing love to others and deferring to their needs and showing strength and truth in our actions.

- Read Matthew 7:15–23 and think through areas in which we need to be wise and stand for truth, and areas in which we need to show love.

Stand for the Truth	Show Love and Compassion

MY RELATIONSHIP TO CHRIST

For each of the following principles, give a personal example of a time when the principle would have applied to your life.

- Resist not evil: _____

_____

_____

_____

_____

- Lay up treasures in heaven: _____

_____

_____

_____

_____

- Give and it shall be given unto you: _____

_____

_____

_____

_____

TEACHER'S LESSON NOTES

Surface _____ : what others see

Surface _____ :
what I am thinking and feeling
inside that others cannot see

Root _____

Root _____ :
Lack of _____

_L E S S O N   T H I R T E E N_

JESUS, THE MASTER TEACHER

Although Jesus was the master teacher of all ages, he was not primarily a teacher. His call was not to teach but to bring His people with Him into the kingdom of God. However, in order to reach His objective, He did a great deal of teaching. Like the sower in one of His parables that we will study, Jesus scattered the good seed wherever and however possible.

THE PARABLE OF THE SOWER

The first parable we are going to study is found in Luke 8:5–15. Read the parable, filling in the chart below as you do so. As you study, consider your life and how the seed of God's Word has affected your own life.

Where Was the Seed Sown?	What Happened to the Seed?	What Did This Mean?
Verse 5: along the path	Verse 5: it was trampled underfoot + birds devoured it	Verse 12: people who have heard but devil takes the word away fr. their hearts so they may not believe + be saved
Verse 6: fell a the rock	Verse 6: it withered b/c it had no moisture	Verse 13: those who have no root — in a time of testing they fall away

With Luke 8:4–15

↓

How do you get roots?

Verse 7:	Verse 7:	Verse 14:
among the thorns	the thorns grew up around it and choked it	they are those who hear but as they go on their way they are choked by the cares, riches and pleasures of life
Verse 8:	Verse 8:	Verse 15:
good soil grew up + yeilded 100 fold	→	those who, hearing the word, hold fast in a honest and good heart and bear fruit with patience

- Be honest! Which of the four examples of seed are you most like? Why do you think so? _____

  _____

  _____

- What did you personally learn from this parable, and how did it help you?

  _____

  _____

PARABLES OF THE KINGDOM

Parable	The Lesson
Parable of the wheat and tares (Matt. 13:24–30) Jesus explains Mt 13:36 -	weeds + wheat will grow together until the harvest then parted
Parable of the mustard seed (Matt. 13:31–32)	small seed big fruit

Parable of the leaven (Matt. 13:33)	*gospel spreads*
Parable of the pearl of great price (Matt. 13:45–46)	*sell all wethes to buy the ~~field~~ pearl*
Parable of the net and the fish (Matt. 13:47–50)	*all here — at judgmt all srted*

THE THEME OF HIS TEACHING—THE KINGDOM OF GOD

- The idea of the kingdom of God was of primary concern in Jesus' teaching. In His first sermon in Mark 1:15, what did He say about the kingdom? _____

_____

_____

- As you have probably noticed in the parables you have read, many of them begin with the words, "The kingdom of heaven (God) is like . . ." Jesus also stated in Matthew 6:33 that the true aim of life is that people should . . ." _____
  But seek first the kingdom of and his righteousness and all these things will be added to you. "

THE KINGDOM IS ALREADY HERE

Jesus did not define what He meant by the kingdom, yet you cannot read the Word without seeing His ideas. Jesus taught that God wanted to rule the hearts of people rather than be the judge of the nations. It was an internal kingdom rather than an external kingdom.

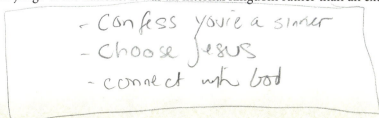

- Confess you're a sinner
- Choose Jesus
- connect with God

- Read Luke 17:20–21 and explain what Jesus said about the presence of the kingdom of God. _____

_____

- Then, in Matthew 7:21, Jesus spoke of a citizen of the kingdom as . . .

_____

THE KINGDOM IS YET TO COME

Jesus also thought of the kingdom as coming in the future. He taught that the true glory of God's kingdom was yet to come and would not be complete until He came again. Jesus also made it very clear that no person or group could build the kingdom. It was God and God alone that would make the kingdom.

- Read Revelation 11:15 and explain how this kingdom is described.

_____

_____

_____

Reread each of the five parables we looked at in Matthew 13 and list each parable under the type of kingdom it is discussing.

The Kingdom Already Here

1. _____

2. _____

3. _____

The Kingdom Yet to Come

1. _____

2. _____

The House on the Rock

This story is usually well known to us by the time we are in junior high. As we have learned, each part of the story is symbolic of some aspect of our lives.

- Read through the story once again in Matthew 7:24–27 and consider what each of the following represents.

  - House _____

  - A rock _____

  - Sand _____

  - Rains, floods, wind _____

- Now rewrite the story, not using the symbols but the true concepts that the story stands for to explain its true meaning. _____

  _____

  _____

  _____

MY RELATIONSHIP TO CHRIST

- Apply some of the parables we have studied to your own life by answering the following questions.

  - Are you one of the wheat or the tares? How do you know? _____

    _____

    _____

  - Has the leaven of the gospel taken hold in your heart and life and begun to change you? How do you know? _____

    _____

    _____

  - Are you more concerned about securing the pearls of this world or the Pearl of Great Price? How do you show this by your life? _____

    _____

    _____

TEACHER'S LESSON NOTES

HOW JESUS TAUGHT

- Taught _____

- Suited His teaching to _____

- Taught by _____

- Taught by _____

THE DEITY OF JESUS CHRIST

At the beginning of our study of the life of Christ, we saw the truth that Jesus is God based on what the Scriptures teach regarding his preexistence. We learned that Jesus was the Creator who was made flesh. He is the Alpha and Omega—the beginning and the end. Jesus has always existed.

We also learned that we can know that Jesus is God because of the fulfillment of hundreds of Old Testament prophecies that foretold the details of Jesus' birth, life, and death. The fact that Jesus fulfilled every prophecy to the minutest detail shows us His deity.

But there are still many other things that show us that Jesus is the one true God.

Jesus proved that He was God while He was on the earth in two major ways: by the words that He spoke and by the works which He did.

THE WORDS HE SPOKE

Show His Authority

From the time that Jesus taught the scribes in the temple when He was only twelve years old, it was obvious that Jesus was One who had authority beyond earthly understanding. As you look up the following verses, explain how others viewed His authority.

Verses	What Was Taking Place	How Others Viewed His Authority
Luke 2:41–47		

Matthew 7:28–29		
Mark 1:21–27		

- The authority that Jesus evidenced shows His omnipotence. Find the definition of *omnipotence* and write its meaning here. _____

  _____

- How did Jesus show that He was omnipotent?_____

  _____

  _____

Jesus foretold many future events that would happen. Usually He told these things to His disciples. Since the events did occur, we know that His own foreknowledge of these things shows His deity; for no one but God knows the future.

- Look up each of the following verses and explain what Jesus foretold about His own future.

  - Mark 8:31 _____

    _____

    _____

  - John 6:64 _____

    _____

    _____

- John 7:33 _____

  _____

  _____

- John 16:16 _____

  _____

  _____

- John 18:4 _____

  _____

  _____

- This foreknowledge shows the omniscience of Jesus Christ. Find *omniscience* in the dictionary and write its meaning here._____

- How did Jesus evidence omniscience in His ministry? _____

  _____

  _____

  _____

Show He Was One with the Father

Many times Jesus also said that He and the Father were one Person.

- Read each of the verses below and write the phrase that Jesus uses to explain this relationship with His Father.

  - John 10:30 _____

  - John 10:38 _____

  - John 14:10 _____

  - John 17:11 _____

  - John 17:22 _____

The Works He Did

Power over Nature and Demons

Jesus showed many times that He had dominion and power over all of nature and over the world of Satan. All the forces of nature had to submit to His will. Also, all the forces of evil, the demons and devils, had to submit to Him. Read the passages below and explain each story, showing how Jesus evidenced power over each area.

Power over Nature	Power over Demons
Matt. 9:18–19, 23–26:	Matt. 9:32–33:
Matt. 9:20–22:	Matt. 12:22:
Matt. 9:27–31:	

- How does this power show that Jesus is God? _____

_____

_____

Power over Sickness and Death

The many miracles that Jesus did in healing those who had been afflicted or near death also affirmed His deity, for no one could have the power to do these things unless they were God.

- Read each of the following and tell who was healed and the infirmity or disease of which they were healed.

  - Matthew 8:5–13 _____

    _____

  - Matthew 9:18–19, 23–26 _____

    _____

- Matthew 9:20–22 _____

  _____

- Matthew 9:27–31 _____

  _____

- Mark 1:29–31 _____

  _____

- Luke 7:12–16 _____

  _____

- To fully see the truth of what we have been studying, read 1 Corinthians 8:6 several times. Then paraphrase the verse in your own words to show you understand its meaning. _____

  _____

  _____

  _____

MY RELATIONSHIP TO CHRIST

We discussed two basic ways in which Jesus proved that He was God: by the words He spoke and by the works He did. Which of the two has the greater impact on your life?

- Why is this so? _____

  _____

  _____

- Why is the teaching that Jesus is God such an important and basic truth to your life? Does it make a difference to you? Why? _____

  _____

  _____

  _____

  _____

TEACHER'S LESSON NOTES

SEVEN PROOFS OF CHRIST'S DEITY (JOHN 5)

- My Father works, and _____ (5:17–18)

- I can do _____ of Myself (5:19)

- The Father shows the Son _____ (5:20)

- The Father and the Son are _____ (5:21)

- _____ the Son as you honor the Father (5:22–23)

- The Son gives _____ (3:24–26)

- The Son has power over _____ (5:27–29)

FOUR WITNESSES OF CHRIST'S DEITY (JOHN 5)

1. _____ (5:32–35)

2. _____ (5:36)

3. _____ (5:37–38)

4. _____ (5:39–47)

GROWING OPPOSITION

[handwritten: Capernaum / Nain]

[handwritten: Will: Pickup]

☐ map reference

[handwritten: Lumo]

☐ watch Luke 7:1-17 *[handwritten marks]*

[handwritten left margin: O why doesn't He heal everyone today?]

We read the story of the widow's son who was raised to life by Jesus.

- Read Luke 7:15–17 and find the effect of such miracles on the people.

  [handwritten: They were all filled with awe and praised God. "A great prophet has appeared among us God has come to help his people + News spread]

- How far reaching was this effect? *[handwritten: (v.17) throughout Judea and surrounding country side.]*

- Review again the following verses and then explain the impact that Jesus had on the people: Matthew 4:23–25; 8:1, 34; Mark 2:15; John 6:1–2.

  [handwritten: → news spread from Galilee to all over Syria + many who followed him - great crowd followed the all who were ill, in pain, possessed, seizing, paralysed large crowds followed him and came to meet him + pleaded with him to have — large crowds followed him came to him from Galilee, Jerusalem, The Decapolis, Judea, and the region across the Jordan. and he healed them.]

JESUS PROVES HIS DEITY TO JOHN

We have previously studied the opposition to Jesus by the Pharisees because of His claim to be the Son of God. Because they thought of this as a blasphemous remark, they wanted to stop Jesus from having any further impact on the people.

Jesus also claimed to have authority over the Old Testament laws and was saying that the needs of the people were more important than the laws of the Pharisees. This further angered the religious leaders.

Now Jesus is discussing the testimony and life of John the Baptist, and a few religious leaders are listening.

- Some men who were disciples of John the Baptist came to see who Jesus was. To prove His deity, what did Jesus do according to Luke 7:21? _Cured many who had diseases, sickness, and evil spirits, and gave sight to many who were blind_

JESUS HAS THE POWER TO FORGIVE – _eat at Simon's house_

We have seen the growing popularity of Jesus among the common people. But we have also learned in past lessons that the Pharisees had been alarmed at the teachings of Jesus and had begun to think of ways to eliminate Him so He would no longer have an impact on the people.

One Pharisee, after hearing Him discuss John the Baptist, invited Jesus to his home to eat. Read the story of what happened in Luke 7:36–50.

Luke video Luke 7:36-50

- Who came to the house to see Jesus, and what did she do to show her love for Him? _A woman in that town who lived a sinful life alabaster jar of perfume stood behind him at his feet weeping – wet his feet with her tears + wiped them with her hair – poured kissed them and perfume on them_

- Why was the Pharisee upset at this, and what did he think Jesus should have done to the woman? _If this man were a prophet he would know who is touching him that she is a sinner   not have her touch him_

- Explain the parable that Jesus shared with the Pharisee. _one owed lots \ both one owed little / forgiven forgiven lots loves more_

- What point was He making? _She knows she is desperate for me so she worships + loves like crazy you don't know you're sinned – you do not show love to me_

94

- Then Jesus compared the Pharisee's attitude toward Him with the woman's attitude. What primary difference was He pointing out? _____

  she knows she been forgiven

- The woman's faith in Jesus and love for Him saved her. How did the Pharisee and those with him react according to verse 49? _____

  "who is this who even forgives sins?"

JESUS REBUKES THE PHARISEES

Another time Jesus was invited to eat at the home of another Pharisee. The details of this situation are found in Luke 11:37–54.

- Always looking for a reason to criticize Him, why did the Pharisee reprimand Jesus? _he did not wash before the meal_

- Jesus then began to rebuke all of the religious leaders for their attitudes and ways. Beginning with verse 39, list the reasons Jesus gave them for their uncleanness.

  - Reason 1 (11:39–40): _full of greed and wickedness_

  - Reason 2 (11:42): _neglect justice and the love of God_

  - Reason 3 (11:43): _love the most important seats in the synagogue and respectful greetings in the marketplace_

- Reason 4 (11:44): _Unmarked graves - people walk over w/out knowing it_

- Reason 5 (11:46): _load people with burdens they can't carry and you do not help them_

- Reason 6 (11:47–48): _kill the prophets + approve of those who do_

- What did Jesus say would be the result of these things according to verses 49–52?
I will send them prophets and apostles some they will kill and others they will persecute (teachers of the law)

- How did the scribes and Pharisees respond to the things Jesus had said to them?
began to oppose him fiercely and besiege him with questions - waiting to catch him in what he might say

READ ONLY

The key concept in this section is the importance of heart attitudes, not just external life and actions. The Pharisees continually brought up the laws, the rules, and the traditions of what people should do out of duty to God. Jesus did not focus on the external duties of the law. He wanted people to focus on their inner attitudes. He knew that if a person is right on the inside, right outward actions will follow.

- How did He try to get this point across to the Pharisees in the above passage?
tough love?

- Why do you think that the Pharisees were not able to grasp what Jesus was saying to them? _They were prideful_

WHAT JESUS SAW IN THE PHARISEES

Jesus was trying to help the religious leaders by exposing them as they truly were. These people were so conscious of the external display of righteousness that they failed to understand that true righteousness begins on the inside. As you read each of the following verses, indicate which of these characteristics of false (only external) righteousness is being discussed: hypocrisy, a judgmental attitude toward others, self-righteousness, outward display of religion, and legalism.

Stephen

Verse	Characteristic of False Righteousness
Jeremiah 2:35	Self-righteousness
Matthew 6:5	legalism
Matthew 7:3	a judgmental attitude
Matthew 23:23	outward display of religion
John 7:23	hypocrisy?

WHY THE PHARISEES OPPOSED JESUS

We have discussed several reasons for the growing opposition of the Pharisees and other religious leaders against Jesus.

- Review the lesson and list the reasons that have been brought out.

  - Reason One: _His claims to be "Son of God."_

  - Reason Two: _They wanted to stop Him from having any more impact on the people_

  - Reason Three: _His claims to have authority over the Old Testament laws (needs of people more imp. than laws of pharisees)_

X

- Reason Four: _They were convicted by His_

- Reason Five: _They were self-righteous_

- Knowing human nature and the attitudes and feelings of people who are not walking with God, why do you think the Pharisees and other religious leaders were so against Jesus? _He offended them_

- Do you think the reasons that they gave verbally were really valid in their minds, or do you think they were blinded in any way? _____ _blinded_

MY RELATIONSHIP TO CHRIST

Considering the attitudes of the Pharisees toward Jesus, what must we learn about our own judgments toward others?

- What problems within ourselves must we guard against as we consider our attitudes toward others? _Self-righteousness, outward_

TEACHER'S LESSON NOTES

Jealousy
Anger
Covetousness

→ Critical,
fault-finding
spirit

→ Hatred
Bitterness

→ Murder

JESUS, THE BREAD OF LIFE

Of all the miracles of Jesus, the feeding of the five thousand is the only one recorded by all four gospels. As you study this miracle and then the material in reference to Jesus being the "bread of life," consider why this miracle holds such a prominent place in the Scriptures.

THE PROBLEM

In John 6:1–4, we see that Jesus went up into the mountains to be alone with His disciples.

- Why did He do this?_____

  _____

- Soon they were interrupted. According to verses 5–7, what took place, and with what problem were Jesus and the disciples confronted? _____

  _____

- What did Jesus ask Philip, and why do you think He asked him this? _____

  _____

  _____

- How did Philip respond, and what does this show us about Philip at this point in his relationship to Jesus? _____

  _____

  _____

  _____

- How does this passage indicate the immense popularity Jesus had with the people?

  _____

  _____

  _____

THE SOLUTION

- Andrew had a different response than did Philip. What did he tell Jesus in verses 8–9, and what do you think his attitude was about the solution? _____

_____

_____

In verses 10–13, Jesus solved the problem. Read these verses and list the things that Jesus told the disciples and the people to do. In order for the miracle to take place, everyone had to simply obey what He told them to do. Often, obedience is the key to overcoming problems.

What They Were Told to Do

- _____

- _____

- _____

How They Responded

- _____

- _____

- _____

THE RESPONSE

Immediately after the miracle was completed and everyone had eaten until they were filled, Jesus departed.

- According to verses 14–15, why do you think He did this? _____

_____

_____

The disciples had seen a great blessing. A wonderful miracle had taken place, and we can be sure that Philip and Andrew and all the others that were there grew stronger in their faith because of what they saw. But it was that very evening that the faith of the disciples was again tested. Read John 6:16–21 and discern how they responded this time. As you read, explain what the immediate problem was, what test you believe Jesus was putting before them, how the problem was solved, and finally, what lesson Jesus wanted them to learn.

- The Problem: _____
  _____

- The Test: _____
  _____

- The Solution: _____
  _____

- The Lesson: _____
  _____

In Matthew 14:24–33, we see another account of the story. What happened between Peter and the Lord? Why did Peter succeed at first, and what then caused him to fail?

- What lesson did Jesus want Peter to learn? _____
  _____
  _____
  _____
  _____
  _____

THE IMPORTANCE OF THE MIRACLE

As we began the lesson, we recognized that this miracle was very important because it is the only one recorded in all four gospels. Why do you think it holds such importance?

- _____
- _____
- _____
- _____

JESUS, THE BREAD OF LIFE

After the great miracle of the feeding of the five thousand, Jesus went into the synagogue at Capernaum and began to preach. First He made a very important statement to the people which showed them what was in their hearts.

- Why did Jesus say they came after Him according to John 6:26?

  _____

  _____

Then Jesus began to explain in yet another way who He was and why He had been sent by the Father. This is the great discourse to explain that He is the true bread that was sent to fill their every need. Read the following verses closely and explain what Jesus says concerning the true bread.

Verses	What Is Said About the True Bread
John 6:32	
John 6:33	
John 6:35	
John 6:47–48	
John 6:49–51	

Just before Jesus went to the cross, He had supper with His disciples for the last time. In a room that was set aside and quiet, He shared the Lord's Supper with them. Read what happened during this supper in Matthew 26:26–29 and Mark 14:22–24. Then read John 6:53–58.

- What similarities do you find between these passages? How was the Last Supper symbolic of what Jesus taught in John 6? _____

  _____

  _____

  _____

FOUR PROMISES OF THE TRUE BREAD

As you review the above verses, you will see that Jesus made four promises regarding the true bread. Review the verses given below and write what is promised to those who believe on Christ as the true bread.

- Promise One (6:35): _____

- Promise Two (6:50–51, 58): _____

- Promise Three (6:54): _____

- Promise Four (6:56): _____

CONTINUED OPPOSITION

The multitudes, just as Jesus had said, loved to watch His miracles and see the healings. They also enjoyed most of what He had to say in His preaching. But a message such as this concerned many. They did not understand His meaning and were unwilling to listen and learn with their hearts.

- What upset the Jews? (vs. 52) _____

  _____

- What did many of His disciples think? (vv. 60–61, 66) _____

  _____

  _____

- How did a few of these followers feel in their hearts? (vs. 64) _____

  _____

- How did the twelve disciples react? (vv. 67–71) _____

  _____

  _____

MY RELATIONSHIP TO CHRIST

What aspects of this lesson have been difficult for you to understand? Obedience and faith work together as we have seen. We can have faith in God, but if we do not act accordingly in obedience, we will never see the results of faith. To see the miracles of the fish and loaves, the disciples had to do what Jesus told them to do.

• Give an example from your own life in which you obeyed the Lord and saw Him work in a special way. _____

_____

_____

_____

TEACHER'S LESSON NOTES

THE TRUE BREAD

Characteristics of the True Bread

• A _____

• Gives _____

• _____

Facts About Bread

• It is a _____

• It is needed _____

REVIEW

KEY PEOPLE

Fill in the blanks below using the following words:

Matthew	Elijah	Zacharias	Andrew
Satan	Adam and Eve	Elisabeth	John the Baptist
Herodias's daughter	The rich young man	The woman at the well	Nicodemus
Peter	The Pharisees	The nobleman	

- _____ called Christ the "Lamb of God" and proclaimed His coming.

- _____ were given the first promise of the Savior.

- At first, the religious leaders thought Jesus might be the prophet named _____.

- _____ was responsible for the death of John the Baptist.

- _____ was the mother of John the Baptist.

- _____ fell because he wanted more power than God.

- Jesus taught _____ about "living water."

- _____ was the disciple who was a publican (tax collector).

- _____ could not speak until his son was born because he didn't believe God.

- _____ was a Pharisee who came to learn more about Jesus at night.

- _____ did not think Jesus should eat with sinners.

- _____'s son was healed without Jesus' presence.

- Jesus told _____ to let down his nets, and two ships were filled with fish.

- _____ is a symbol of those who do not receive Christ because the things of this world are too important to them.

- _____ was the disciple who told Jesus about the boy with the loaves and fish, showing faith in God.

IMPORTANT TERMS

Fill In the blanks below using the following words:

the true bread	pearl of great price	Pool of Bethesda	water
Alpha and Omega	omnipotent	fisherman	Beatitudes
Word	leaven	temple	Lamb of God
Passover	testament	scribes	Passover lamb
Pharisees	born again	publican	I am
omniscience	prophecy	rock	

- Two names for Jesus that mean He has always existed: _____ _____

- Name for Jesus that means He is our Passover sacrifice: _____

- God created all things by the _____

- The term meaning that Jesus is our strong foundation: _____

- The term that emphasizes that Jesus has all power and uses it to care for us and meet all our needs: _____

- A picture or type of sin: _____

- An animal without blemish or spot—a picture of Jesus: _____

- Passages that told the future details of Jesus' life: _____

- A word meaning "a promise of God": _____

- Jesus drove moneychangers out of the temple during this time: _____

- In referring to Himself with this symbol, Jesus said He would be "rebuilt" in three days: _____

- The term Jesus used with Nicodemus to explain salvation: _____

- The word meaning a tax collector: _____

- Teachers of the law: _____

- Jesus used this symbol to reach the woman at the well about new life in Him: _____

- At this place, a man who had been infirmed for 38 years picked up his bed and walked: _____

- The occupation of most of the disciples: _____

MULTIPLE CHOICE

Check the box with the correct answer to each of the following.

- The parables of the lost sheep and the lost coin both teach

  ☐ that we should be careful with what God has given us.

  ☐ that we should keep all things in order.

  ☐ that Jesus wants each individual to be saved.

- Nicodemus was

  - ☐ a roman soldier.

  - ☐ a Pharisee.

  - ☐ a political ruler.

- Jesus showed His omniscience to the Samaritan woman when

  - ☐ He traveled through Samaria.

  - ☐ He taught her about the living water.

  - ☐ He told her about her five husbands.

- The Pharisees were upset that the disciples plucked corn because

  - ☐ they did this on the Sabbath.

  - ☐ they were taking food from the poor.

  - ☐ they were stealing from the owner.

- Commitment, faithfulness, and discipleship are all aspects of the character trait

  - ☐ faith.

  - ☐ loyalty.

  - ☐ compassion.

- The scribes and Pharisees said Jesus blasphemed God because

  - ☐ He healed people and performed miracles.

  - ☐ He claimed to be God.

  - ☐ He performed miracles on the Sabbath.

- A principle tells us

  - ☐ what our duty is.

  - ☐ what our inner attitudes and motives should be.

  - ☐ rules to live by.

- The principle of focusing on our relationship with God more than accumulating material goods was taught in the Sermon on the Mount with the words

- [ ] resist not evil.
- [ ] lay up treasures in heaven.
- [ ] give and it will be given unto you.

• The root cause of life's problems is always

- [ ] the problems we have in our lives.
- [ ] our feelings.
- [ ] a lack of trust in God.

• The parable of the sower and the seed teaches

- [ ] what effect God's Word has had in our lives.
- [ ] the need to do all things consistently.
- [ ] the principle of sowing and reaping.

Check the correct answer for each of the following.

• The first miracle took place in

- [ ] Nazareth
- [ ] Jerusalem
- [ ] Cana

• John the Baptist baptized believers in the

- [ ] Jordan River
- [ ] Red Sea
- [ ] Sea of Galilee

• Nazareth was located in

- [ ] Galilee
- [ ] Samaria
- [ ] Judea

• Jerusalem was located in

- [ ] Galilee
- [ ] Samaria
- [ ] Judea

• Each year Jesus traveled to attend the Passover in

- [ ] Bethlehem
- [ ] Cana
- [ ] Jerusalem

• The Jews hated the people of

- [ ] Galilee
- [ ] Samaria
- [ ] Judea

- Jesus met the woman at the well in

  ☐ Cana   ☐ Sychar   ☐ Capernaum

- All the disciples except Judas came from

  ☐ Galilee   ☐ Nazareth   ☐ Judea

- Jesus faced rejection by the people of

  ☐ Nazareth   ☐ Capernaum   ☐ Bethany

- The names of the three provinces were Galilee, Samaria, and

  ☐ Jerusalem   ☐ Judea   ☐ Nazareth

SHORT ANSWERS

- Give five reasons for the Pharisees' growing opposition against Jesus.

  _____

  _____

  _____

  _____

  _____

- Why didn't Jesus allow either rejection or popularity to have an effect on Him?

  _____

  _____

  _____

- What is the theme of Jesus' teaching? _____

- What was the basic difference between what the Pharisees focused on and what Jesus focused on?

  _____

  _____

  _____

- The miracles that Jesus did showed His power over what four things?

  _____

  _____

- What four promises did Jesus make to those who would believe on Him as the true bread?

  _____

  _____

  _____

  _____

THE MIGHTY WORKS OF JESUS

The complete and full power of the Creator God flowed through Jesus, manifesting itself in great and mighty works and miracles. We have seen that everywhere Jesus went the streets were soon lined with those who had need of healing as well as others who were simply curious. Many, many people, seeing the miracles, knew that God was with them. They praised God and glorified Him for the things that Jesus did. But we have also seen that in nearly every crowd there were also the enemies of Jesus, the religious leaders, whose purpose it was to find fault.

DIFFERENT MIRACLES AND DIFFERENT RESPONSES

Verses	What Happened?	What Jesus Did or Said	Response to Jesus
Matt. 15:21–28 Mark 7:24–30			
Matt. 15:29–31			

what happened? what Jesus said or did? Response to Jesus?

Matt. 15:32–38 Mark 8:1–9			
Mark 8:22–26			
Matt. 17:14–21 Mark 9:14–27 Luke 9:37–43			
Luke 13:10			
Luke 17:11–19			
Matt. 20:29–34			

- There were many more miracles that Jesus did than are recorded in the Bible. What does Matthew 9:35–36 explain concerning this? _____

_____

_____

_____

_____

_____

_____

IMPORTANT ASPECTS OF JESUS' MIRACULOUS WORKS

- Luke 10:8–12—What were the disciples to tell the people when they healed the sick?

  _____

  _____

- How were they to act if they were not welcomed? _____

  _____

  _____

- Luke 7:20–23—Jesus did works of power that no one else had ever done. When John the Baptist's disciples came to Jesus asking if He were the Messiah, he said . . .

  _____

  _____

  _____

  _____

  _____

- John 9:1–5—Jesus healed a man who had been blind since birth. Many of His followers asked if the man was born blind because of sin in either his life or his parents' life. How did Jesus respond to this? _____

  _____

  _____

  _____

- Matthew 8:5–10, 13—Here Jesus healed the servant of a centurion soldier. What did Jesus notice about the centurion that impressed Him? _____

  _____

  _____

  _____

- Look over each of the above answers to this section and come to some conclusions regarding Jesus' attitude toward the people that He helped. _____

  _____

  _____

  _____

  _____

  _____

NO MIRACLES FOR UNWORTHY PURPOSES

Today, people are continually looking for greater thrills and ways to find pleasure. New films of daring are sought out to fill a need for new thrills. There were people in the days of Jesus who were also looking for something unusual or different. But Jesus refused to work miracles like a magician who performs his bag of tricks. Often Jesus said to those whom He healed, "See that you say nothing to anyone," for His miracles were not just to attract attention.

We are going to look at several passages of Scripture that discuss people's desire and curiosity to see a sign and Jesus' reaction to this.

- As a review of Jesus' first attack from Satan in this area, what miracles did Satan tempt Jesus to perform? (Matt. 4:1–7) _____

  _____

  _____

  _____

- Who asked for a sign in Matthew 12:38–39 and then in Matthew 16:1–4?

  _____

- What was Jesus' response, and how did He refer to these people?

  _____

  _____

  _____

- Again in Mark 8:10–12, the Pharisees again came asking for a sign. How did Jesus respond to them this time?_____

  _____

- Why do you think the Scriptures say that He sighed deeply? _____

  _____

- Read Luke 11:15–20 and 28–30. How did some of the people think He had cast out demons? _____

- How did Jesus dispute this? _____

  _____

  _____

- What sign was given to this generation as Jonah was given to the last generation?

  _____

- Why did Jesus call this an evil generation? _____

  _____

  _____

- Later, in Luke 16:31, what did Jesus say about their faith in signs?

  _____

  _____

  _____

- Jesus summed up the attitudes toward the people of this generation in John 4:48. Copy His words here and consider whether or not these words apply to you.

  _____

  _____

Jesus wanted His followers to simply trust in the words He spoke to them and the holy life He lived before them. If they would not believe the testimony He spoke and lived, no miracle would help.

MY RELATIONSHIP TO CHRIST

- Consider your own attitude to the Lord. Do you need signs and miraculous works to have faith in Him, or do you believe based on His words and the testimony of His life? _____

The truth is that when we have accepted the truth of Jesus by faith, He shows us in many ways that He is working in our lives. Often we even see miraculous things happening.

- Write a paragraph below explaining some of the evidences God has given you that He is truly at work in your life. _____

_____

_____

_____

_____

_____

_____

_____

TEACHER'S LESSON NOTES

WHY JESUS PERFORMED MIRACLES

- Jesus had _____ on people

- To show the _____ and _____ of God

- It was one of the marks of the _____

CONDITIONS NECESSARY FOR MIRACLES

- Perfect _____ in His heavenly Father

- Faith in _____

- The _____ of God

CONFUSION AND DIVISION CONCERNING JESUS

AT THE FEAST OF TABERNACLES

The Feast of Tabernacles is approaching, and Jesus' brothers want Him to go to Jerusalem to attend the feast.

- Read John 7:1–8 and explain the reasons His brothers wanted Him to go and why He did not want to go with them.

Why His Brothers Wanted Him to Go	Why He Did Not Want to Go

- What did Jesus do according to verses 9 and 10? _____
  _____
  _____
  _____

REGULATIONS REGARDING THE FEAST

In the Book of Leviticus in the Old Testament, God had used Moses to explain the regulations for the Feast of Tabernacles. The Jews celebrated this feast to offer thanks for the harvest of grain, fruit, wine, and oil and as a reminder of being taken out of Egypt by God. Read Leviticus 23:34–44 and explain the following details about this feast.

- When did it take place? _____

- How long did it last? _____

- What were some peculiar customs of the feast?_____

  _____

  _____

  _____

  _____

- What were the reasons for the customs? _____

  _____

  _____

  _____

  _____

CONFUSION CONCERNING JESUS

Jesus does go into the temple to teach near the end of the feast. As He talks to the people, it is obvious that a negative attitude is building toward Him. Read John 7:11–31 together as a class, noting the verses indicated below. Then focus in on these verses and explain on the chart who is talking about Jesus.

Next, under the positive or negative column, tell what is being said about Jesus or the attitude that is coming from the people. We must remember that Jesus will not die for another six months. Even though the timing is not yet ready for the Son of God to be crucified, things are happening that will surely bring all of this to pass.

John 7	Who Is Talking?	Positive?	Negative?
12			
15			

20			
23			
25			
26			
27			
30			
31			

- Finally the Pharisees decide to take action. What did they try to have done, and how did they go about it? (John 7:32) _____

- But Jesus confused them with a very important comment in verses 33–34. What did He say, and what did He mean? _____

_____

_____

_____

_____

- Why were the Jews confused in verse 35? _____

_____

_____

TEACHING ON THE HOLY SPIRIT

During the Feast of Tabernacles, at daybreak each day for seven days, a priest went to the pool of Siloam and filled a golden pitcher with water. He was accompanied by a procession of people and a musical band. On returning to the temple he was welcomed by three blasts of a trumpet. Going to the west side of the great altar, he poured water into a silver basin that had holes in the bottom. The leaking water was carried off, accompanied with songs and shouts from the people and the sound of trumpets.

Then, on the last day of the feast, a very special ceremony took place. The rabbis drew water in a golden vessel from the Pool of Siloam. A priest took the water up through a throng of spectators towards the forecourt of the temple. Entering the temple court by the Water Gate, he moved to the altar where he mixed the clear water with ruddy wine and poured it into two silver cups upon the altar. Then the Levites clanged their cymbals and sounded trumpets while the people sang with joy.

- It was during this particular ceremony that Jesus began to preach about Himself. Obviously this was planned. What did Jesus say about Himself? (vs. 37)

_____

_____

- What was the meaning of what He said in verse 38, and when was this to take place according to verse 39? _____

_____

_____

_____

_____

Jesus again made a very important assertion. He was saying that He was God and that He was a fulfillment of the Feast of Tabernacles celebration just as He was a fulfillment of the Passover Feast. He was the Messiah that had come to fulfill the Old Testament prophecies and laws.

GREAT DIVISION CONCERNING JESUS

We can be sure that Jesus was the topic of conversation in most households. People wondered at the things He was saying about Himself. More and more often, the people were divided in their opinions. Many believed He was a great prophet sent from God, but they did not accept that He was God. Read the following verses closely and try to find a picture of the division that had developed among the people.

John 7	What Did They Think?	What Was the Confusion?
40–41		
42–43		
44		
45–49		
50–53		

Jesus had brought about all of this because of the words that He had spoken. Certainly Jesus was not ignorant or confused. Why do you think He wanted the confusion and division to develop? _____

_____

_____

MY RELATIONSHIP TO CHRIST

All of us are faced with situations that cause us to have to make choices regarding our attitudes and stands as Christians. Consider your stand for Christ over the past few months. What types of situations bring confusion into your mind? Where does the confusion arise? What choices are placed before you? How can you respond in a stronger way the next time it happens? _____

_____

_____

_____

_____

_____

TEACHER'S LESSON NOTES

LEARNING TO MAKE RIGHT DECISIONS

Deciding to _____

Deciding to _____

- _____ in your heart

- Make decisions _____ you face temptation

Deciding to _____

- Right _____ form right _____

- Maturity involves taking _____ for personal decisions

Making right decisions

- Receive good _____ and _____

- Decisions must be based on _____

- Your decisions and convictions must come from _____

LESSONS ON HUMILITY

One of the greatest lessons that Jesus came to teach concerning how to live our lives was in regard to our attitudes toward others. Many called Jesus by the term "Master" or "rabbi", which means teacher. These terms were used of those deserving of the highest honor and respect. Obviously our Lord deserved to be called by names denoting great respect.

- Read Isaiah 9:6 and list other terms or ideas that show that Christ is truly deserving of great honor and respect.

  - _____
  - _____
  - _____
  - _____
  - _____

No one who has ever lived deserves the honor and respect that Jesus does. For the reasons given above plus the fact that He is the Creator God who made us shows that no one deserves praise and honor and glory as He does. And yet He came to live on the earth to show us another way.

- Write a short paragraph to explain how He lived while He was on the earth.

  _____
  _____
  _____
  _____
  _____
  _____
  _____

Jesus instead showed us that humility and servanthood are a better way to live our lives. Jesus did not come to exalt Himself, but to minister to us; He came not to be served, but to serve; He came not to be elevated to become a king as so many wanted, but to die on a cross that we might have eternal life.

- Copy Matthew 20:28 to see how Jesus expresses this important truth.

_____

_____

_____

THE DISCIPLES MUST LEARN HUMILITY

It was very difficult even for the twelve chosen disciples to understand this important truth.

- Read Luke 9:46–48 and Matthew 18:1–6. What concern did the disciples have?

_____

_____

- What example did Jesus use to teach them the need for humility?

_____

_____

- Explain in your own words what He taught them through this example.

_____

_____

_____

"EXCEPT YE BECOME AS LITTLE CHILDREN"

Jesus obviously had great regard for the feelings and concerns of little children. People often brought their children to Him just so that they might receive a touch from Him. The disciples, on another occasion, were disturbed at this.

- According to Luke 18:15–16, what did they do, and how did Jesus rebuke them?

_____

_____

- What lesson was He trying to teach again?

  _____

  _____

  _____

- Look up the following verses and find other attitudes that Jesus showed toward children—attitudes that we need to learn.

Verses	Attitudes of Jesus
Matthew 10:42	
Matthew 18:10	
Mark 9:35–37	
Matthew 11:16–17	

- Why do you think Jesus used the example of young children to teach humility?

  _____

  _____

  _____

- What qualities do they have that we can learn from?

  _____

  _____

  _____

  _____

THE PHARISEE AND THE PUBLICAN

Jesus used a parable to compare true humility with self-righteous attitudes.

- Read Luke 18:9–14 and compare the two men.

The Pharisee	The Publican

- What were the purposes and lessons of this parable according to verses 9 and 14?

_____

_____

_____

_____

_____

_____

THE AMBITION OF JAMES AND JOHN

Another time Jesus was approached about this same issue. Read Mark 10:35–45 and answer the following questions.

- Who came to Jesus, and what was their request? _____

_____

_____

- How did Jesus say that authority in the kingdom would be different from those who rule over the Gentiles? _____

_____

_____

_____

MY RELATIONSHIP TO CHRIST

- Whenever our pride or attitudes of selfishness become a part of our thinking and actions, what should we remember from this lesson? _____

  _____

  _____

  _____

TEACHER'S LESSON NOTES

TRUE GREATNESS IS . . .

- _____ God's commandments (Matt. 5:19)

- _____ to others (Matt. 20:26)

- Being the _____ of all (Matt. 23:11)

HOW TO SHOW HUMILITY

- Sit in a place of humility and let others _____
  (Luke 14:10)

- The person who serves others is always _____
  _____ (Luke 22:26)

- We are not to think _____
  than we ought to think (Rom. 12:3)

- We are to submit to _____ and be subject
  _____ (1 Pet. 5:5)

PROMISES FOR THE HUMBLE

- God will _____ (James 4:10)

- God will give _____ to deal with life situations (1 Pet. 5:5)

- God will _____ those who _____ themselves over us (Luke 14:11)

It's impossible
to forgive without
Jesus' work on the cross.

is it hard to forgive?

- Why do we not Ask forgive?

① Think of society/scene (maybe yourself)
   forgive. you want to
② why haven't you?

③ Imagine that sin poured on Jesus
   for cross

verse - nailed to the cross

Jesus - Justice - made right

- punishment -

LESSONS ON FORGIVENESS

It is God's desire that we have a right relationship with every other person that He created. This is obviously very difficult since problems arise between others and us from time to time.

God emphasizes the importance of forgiveness. He knows that true forgiveness in every situation seems impossible. But He gave us Jesus to show us how it can be possible.

Consider that Jesus died for each sin we will commit in our lives. Each of our sins is an abomination to God. Sin shows itself in so many ugly ways that hurt God over and over again. We go against His commandments, we reject Him by ignoring his purpose and plan for us, we forget to acknowledge Him, and we put far too many things ahead of Him in our hearts. Many people curse Him and murder, hate, destroy, lie, and steal from others He created. And yet, His forgiveness is complete and genuine, as we see demonstrated on the cross. We did not deserve His forgiveness, but we have it. There will be many times that you will feel that someone else who has wronged you does not deserve your forgiveness, but you can still forgive through the power of God within you.

As we study this lesson, consider the freedom that forgiveness has brought to you and how forgiving others will continue to give you freedom to live your life fully and without hindrances.

TO SEEK AND SAVE THE LOST

Read Matthew 18:11–14. As you read these verses, explain each of the following in your own words.

- The Example or Parable Used: _____

  _____

  _____

- The Principle Taught: _____

   _____

   _____

- The Purpose of God: _____

Read Matthew 18:21–35 to understand still another principle that Jesus wants us to learn about forgiveness.

- The Example or Parable Used: _____

   _____

   _____

   _____

   _____

   _____

   _____

   _____

   _____

- The Principle Taught: _____

   _____

- The Purpose of God: _____

   _____

PRINCIPLES OF FORGIVENESS

God shows us basic principles on how to deal with others with a forgiving spirit. Matthew 18:15–17 teaches us a series of steps that we need to take when another Christian does something against us. Remember, if that person has sinned, the ultimate goal of this process is to help them restore their relationship with God, not just to "settle your account" with them or to expose their sin to others. Showing love to our brothers and sisters in Christ includes doing what is best for them in their relationship with God.

- Read these verses and describe each step found in Matthew 18:15-17.

Step One: If . . .	Then . . .
Step Two: If . . .	Then . . .
Step Three: If . . .	Then . . .

- For each of the following passages, discern the principle that Jesus is teaching and explain it in your own words.

Verses	Principle of Forgiveness
Matthew 5:38–39	
Matthew 5:41–42	
Matthew 5:44	

Matthew 5:45–46	
Matthew 18:21–22	
Mark 11:25–26	
Luke 17:2	
Luke 17:3	
Luke 17:4	

MY RELATIONSHIP TO CHRIST

- What is one of the primary ways you can judge how strong your relationship with Jesus is? _____

_____

TEACHER'S LESSON NOTES

JESUS CAME TO FORGIVE SINNERS

Jesus Associated with _____

Jesus' Purpose

- To seek and _____ the _____

- To teach that sin includes _____ and not just _____

  - Sin hurts the heart of _____

  - Sin always affects _____

Forgiveness—Jesus' Remedy for Sin

- Jesus taught about a new relationship with _____

- The death of Christ on the cross shows the _____ of God's _____ to win us to Himself

- By receiving _____ as our Savior, we enter into a new _____ with God

What God's Forgiveness Gives Us

- A _____ with God

- _____ with God

- _____ and _____

THE TRUE MEANING OF LOVE

Throughout our study of the life of Christ, we have seen the true meaning of love as evidenced by Jesus Himself. The Pharisees and other religious leaders continually focused on traditions, rites, laws, and rituals. Jesus tried to focus on the needs of the people themselves. He taught self-sacrifice for others and a genuine love that seeks to meet the needs of others and uplift them in their lives. Jesus taught the love of God in action.

Once, a lawyer, listening among many others to the words of Jesus, asked Him what he could do to inherit eternal life. Actually the Bible says the lawyer was tempting Jesus, which shows that the lawyer was trying to trap or trick Jesus into giving an answer that could be used against Him.

- Read Luke 10:25–27. Jesus had the lawyer answer his own question. What was the answer? _____

  _____

  _____

  _____

  _____

- The lawyer then asked a very important question in verse 29. What was the question? _____

- What is the answer to this question? _____

  _____

- Who is your neighbor? _____

EVIDENCES OF LOVE

Read each of the following verses carefully, for in each you will find a principle that God wants you to consider in your attitude toward others. You will find that from God's point of view, there is never a reason not to show love to "your neighbor." Read the verse and state the principle in your own words from a first person viewpoint.

Verse	Principles of Demonstrating Love
Matthew 5:44	
John 13:35	
Romans 12:9	
Romans 13:10	
Romans 15:1	
James 2:8	
1 Thess. 3:12	
1 John 4:12	
1 John 4:20	

THE ADULTEROUS WOMAN

Jesus came under attack and opposition from those who wanted to stop His ministry. He had been accused of blasphemy, deception, and demon possession. More and more, He was under attack for His teachings. Of course, Jesus knew that this was all part of the divine plan that would lead to the cross. Because of the love that He was to show to us, He did not try to sidestep this process. He willingly walked through each situation.

The Pharisees could really find nothing to accuse Him of that was strong enough to have Jesus found guilty of wrongdoing. And so they tried to trap Jesus into a wrong response. Read the story of the woman who had lived in sin in John 8:1–11. In the days of Jesus, the normal punishment for adultery was stoning. As you read, think through each of the following.

- The Trap: The Pharisees tried to trap Jesus by presenting Him with a problem. Explain the situation Jesus dealt with and the problem He faced.

  _____
  _____
  _____
  _____
  _____
  _____

- Jesus' Response: The great wisdom of the Lord was evident. How did Jesus handle the situation, and how did He instead trap the Pharisees?

  _____
  _____
  _____
  _____

- The Pharisees' Response: What did the Pharisees do next?

  _____
  _____

- Jesus' Response to the Woman: How did Jesus respond to the woman after the others left? Did He accept her sin? _____

_____

_____

_____

_____

TWO PARABLES ON LOVE

Jesus taught many times in parables on the subject of how to treat one another. Review the following two parables and give a brief synopsis of each.

The Prodigal Son (Luke 15:11–32)

_____

_____

_____

_____

_____

The Good Samaritan (Luke 10:30–37)

_____

_____

_____

_____

_____

HUMILITY, FORGIVENESS, AND LOVE

Demonstrating love in every situation must of necessity also involve what we have studied in our two previous lessons: humility and forgiveness. Think through the two parables and the situation with the woman taken in adultery and consider different ways in which humility, forgiveness, and love are demonstrated in each. Also mention ways in which these three concepts are not shown.

Story	Humility	Forgiveness	Love
The Adulterous Woman			
The Good Samaritan			
The Prodigal Son			

- Write several sentences that show how humility, forgiveness, and love all must work together in order for us to love and serve others. _____

_____

_____

_____

_____

MY RELATIONSHIP TO CHRIST

- Without mentioning anyone's name, analyze a situation in which you are having difficulty loving someone. As you describe the situation, explain how humility, forgiveness, and love working together will help you to truly love this person.

_____

_____

_____

_____

_____

TEACHER'S LESSON NOTES

THE IGNORANCE OF THE PHARISEES (JOHN 8)

- Ignorance of Christ's _____ (8:13)

- Ignorance of Christ's _____ (8:19)

- Ignorance of Christ's _____ (8:22)

- Ignorance of Christ's _____ (8:25)

- Ignorance of Christ's _____ (8:48)

- Ignorance of Christ's _____ (8:57–58)

- The _____ of their ignorance (8:59)

ANALOGIES OF CHRIST

An analogy is a comparison between two things, people, or ideas. In this lesson, we are going to explore several ways in which God has compared Jesus to common things and experiences of life so that we could more fully understand who Jesus is.

CHRIST, THE GOOD SHEPHERD

When Jesus looked at the people around Him, He saw them as sheep without a shepherd. He declared from the beginning of His ministry that He came to help these people, not to burden them further. "I came not to call the righteous, but sinners to repentance" (Luke 5:32). "The Son of man is come to seek and to save that which was lost" (Luke 19:10).

Of all the creatures that God placed on the earth, the sheep is one of the most timid and helpless creatures and needs the most guidance, protection, and care. Just as the shepherd knows each of his sheep individually, so does Jesus know us individually and is touched with every aspect of our needs. He knows us all by name. He knows the very house in which we live. The distress of each one of us touches His heart. Our cries for help reach His ears. He came to draw everyone unto Himself and to meet our needs in every way.

There are many passages throughout the Scriptures that refer to this picture of Jesus as our shepherd. In each passage, a different aspect of His love and care for us is shown.

- As you read each of the following passages, describe how Jesus ministers to us as the Good Shepherd.

  - Isaiah 40:11 _____
    _____

  - John 10:11 _____
    _____

- Hebrews 13:20 _____
  _____

- 1 Peter 2:25 _____
  _____

- 1 Peter 5:4 _____
  _____

- Psalm 23:1 _____
  _____

- Psalm 23:2 _____
  _____

- Psalm 23:3 _____
  _____

- Psalm 23:4 _____
  _____

ANALOGIES OF THE SHEPHERD

- Read John 10:1–15 together as a class. As your teacher focuses on the following sections of the passage, take notes from the information your teacher gives you.

  - John 10:1, 8, 10 _____
    _____
    _____
    _____

  - John 10:12–13 _____
    _____
    _____
    _____

- John 10:1, 2, 7 _____
  _____
  _____
  _____

- John 10:3–5, 9, 11, 14–15 _____
  _____
  _____
  _____

- Finally, in verse 10, Jesus said, "I am come that they might have life, and that they might have it more abundantly." Based on what you have learned about the Good Shepherd, what do you think the "abundant life" means? _____
  _____
  _____
  _____

CHRIST, THE LIGHT OF THE WORLD

Light has always been a symbol of God's presence. At the creative word in the beginning, light had shone out of darkness. Light had been enshrouded in the pillar of cloud by day and the pillar of fire by night, leading the multitudes of Israelites out of Egypt. Light blazed about the Lord on Mount Sinai. Light rested over the mercy seat in the tabernacle. Light filled the temple of Solomon at its dedication. Light shone on the hills of Bethlehem at nighttime when the angels brought the message of redemption to the watching shepherds. God is light; and Jesus said, "I am the light of the world." Christ declared in still another way His oneness with God.

- As you read each of the following sections of Scripture, explain other aspects of Jesus as the light of the world.

Verse(s)	How the Light Evidences Itself
John 1:4; 8:12 John 1:5	
John 12:35	
2 Corinthians 4:6	
Revelation 21:23; 22:5	

OTHER ANALOGIES USED BY JESUS

Many other common things are used as a comparison to the character or ministry of Jesus. Read each of the following verses, name the analogy, and then explain the meaning of the analogy.

Verse(s)	Analogy	The Comparison to Jesus
John 6:32		
John 14:6		

John 11:25		
Matt. 7:25 1 Cor. 10:4		
John 15:1, 4		

MY RELATIONSHIP TO CHRIST

- Consider each of the analogies we have studied in reference to the character or ministry of Jesus. Which analogy do you most identify with, and why is it important to you? _____

_____

_____

TEACHER'S LESSON NOTES

THE SHEPHERD'S _____

Understanding the _____ problem (9:2–4)

- Not a _____ for sin

- To manifest the _____ of God

The _____ happens (9:6–7)

- The _____ of the miracle

- _____ is essential

JESUS BRINGS _____

- Jesus brings light to the _____ (9:5)

- _____ and _____ bring greater insight into God

- Sight brings _____ (9:34–37)

THE RAISING OF LAZARUS

Among the most faithful of Christ's disciples was Lazarus of Bethany. Lazarus's love for Jesus was deep, and he was greatly beloved by the Savior. It was for Lazarus that the greatest of Christ's miracles was performed. The Savior blessed all who sought His help, but His heart was knit by a strong bond of affection to the family at Bethany. At the home of Lazarus, Jesus had often found rest. Jesus had no home of His own; He was dependent on the hospitality of His friends and disciples. And often, when weary, He found a sincere welcome in this home.

MARY AND MARTHA

Lazarus's two sisters, Mary and Martha, became very important in Jesus' life. As you read the Scripture passages below, consider the difference in the ways they acted and something about the differences in personalities between the two women. Describe what each passage says about these two sisters.

	Luke 10:38–42	John 12:1–8	John 11:20–22, 28–32
Mary			
Martha			

Once, when Jesus visited the home of these friends, a controversy arose between Lazarus's two sisters, Mary and Martha. From Luke 10:38–42, describe what the problem was and what lesson Jesus taught the two women and us about what is important in life. Then in the passage from John, discuss the beautiful lesson that Mary's service to the Lord can teach us.

Luke 10:38–42	John 12:1–8

LAZARUS DIES

Sorrow had entered the peaceful home where Jesus had so often rested. Lazarus was stricken with a sudden illness, and his sisters sent for Jesus. Jesus had left Jerusalem and returned to Perea. He stayed in Perea until He was summoned to Bethany when Lazarus died. At this point, Jesus knew only a very few days were left until His crucifixion.

Recognizing once again that nothing happens by accident in the plan of God, we need to look closely at the details of this great miracle; for it was to foreshadow what would happen to Jesus.

- Read carefully John 11:1–6 and answer the following questions.

    - How did Jesus feel toward this family? _____
    _____

    - What indication can you find that Jesus knew Lazarus would die? _____
    _____
    _____
    _____

    - Did He go immediately to save Lazarus from death? _____

- Why do you think He waited? _____

_____

_____

_____

THE DISCIPLES' WEAKNESSES

After two days, He told His disciples that it was time to return to Judea and to Bethany. As Jesus and His disciples traveled to Lazarus's home, three situations arose in which the disciples still showed a weakness in their spiritual maturity. They obviously still did not totally understand the complete ministry of Jesus.

- What was the disciples' concern in verse 8, and what weakness did this show?

_____

_____

_____

- How did Jesus respond to them in verses 9 and 10? _____

_____

_____

- What misunderstanding did they show in verses 11–14? _____

_____

_____

- What attitude do you think Thomas showed by his statement in verse 16?

_____

JESUS WEPT

We are told in verse 35 that Jesus wept. Review the things we learned about the disciples in verses 8–16, the feelings and attitudes of Mary and Martha in verses 20–32, and the response of the Jews in verse 36.

- Why do you think Jesus was weeping? _____

_____

LAZARUS IS RAISED

Jesus was to evidence His power and control over death and the grave. This mighty miracle was the crowning evidence of the fact that Jesus was truly God and was sent into the world by the Father to be the Savior. It was a demonstration of divine power that should have been sufficient to convince every mind and those who still had questions about His divinity or messiahship. Jesus asked that the stone be removed, and then we see a short conversation between Martha and Jesus (vv. 38–40).

- Why did Jesus reprove Martha? _____
  _____
  _____
  _____

Next, one of the greatest miracles was performed in full view of many witnesses so no one could possibly deny what happened. Read John 11:41–46. Imagine if you were standing with the Jews, the disciples and Mary and Martha watching this great miracle.

- Describe what happened from a first person point of view as if you were in the crowd. _____
  _____
  _____
  _____
  _____
  _____

Many who witnessed the resurrection of Lazarus believed on Jesus and knew that the Messiah had come. But others were so cold in their hearts that they still would not allow their minds and hearts to believe. Their hatred and pride rejected what their eyes had seen. Lazarus had been raised in the full light of day after it was known that he had been in the grave for four days. No one could possibly explain away such evidence. Everyone understood that Satan has no power over life and death and the grave. This could only have been a miracle of God. It is hard to believe then that the hard hearts of the Pharisees grew even harder when they heard of this wonderful happening.

- Read of these reactions in John 11:46–57 and take notes about what the religious leaders thought and did. _____

_____

_____

_____

_____

_____

_____

_____

MY RELATIONSHIP TO CHRIST

Consider once again the attitudes of all the people surrounding Jesus at this time: the disciples, the Jewish people, the religious leaders, Martha, and Mary. Some are confused, some have set their minds to kill Him, some show a lack of faith, and some want only to worship him in every situation.

- Of all these people, whom do you think is the one who is the most willing to follow Jesus at all costs and understands why He should be worshipped? _____

Martha and some of the Jews and disciples had a judgmental attitude toward Mary's obvious devotion to Jesus. Be honest! Are there others that you tend to make judgments about without taking into account differences in personality, interests, or problems that you do not know about?

- Describe the types of judgments you have made about others. _____

_____

_____

- What can you do the next time you begin to do this? _____

_____

_____

TEACHER'S LESSON NOTES

- "I am the _____ and the _____: He that _____ in me, though he were _____, yet shall he _____." (John 11:25)

- The corruptible puts on _____ (1 Cor. 15:53a)

- Mortality puts on _____ (1 Cor. 15:53b)

- Christ abolished _____ (2 Tim. 1:10)

- "God will redeem my _____ from the power of the _____." (Ps. 49:15)

- Believing on Christ gives _____ (John 6:40)

- There will be a _____ for the _____ and the _____ (John 5:28–29)

"THE FULLNESS OF THE TIME" HAD COME

It did not take Satan long in the Garden of Eden to attempt to drive a wedge between God and mankind. Through Satan and Adam's sin, we became captive to sin and death. First Satan had tried to become more powerful than God Himself. When he was thrown out of heaven, he deceived many angels into going with him. Then he began his work of deception on people.

From the very time that sin entered into the world, God promised to provide redemption from the power of sin. Spiritual forces, as well as our own sin nature, try to pervert God's work and subvert God's will. But God is all-knowing and all-powerful, and will accomplish what He desires, regardless of opposition.

When "the fullness of time had come," Jesus became human—though still fully God—to be the perfect sacrifice and rescue our souls. Despite opposition from the time Jesus was born (such as Herod's attempt to kill Jesus), God protected Him in order to carry out His divine plan.

There is no greater threat to Satan than Jesus, so when Jesus went into the desert at the beginning of His ministry, Satan launched a great attack tempting Him to sin. Christ must live a perfect life in order to be a flawless sacrifice. He was the only one who could pay the price for sin. So Jesus resisted Satan's attacks. Just before He went to the cross, Jesus said that the prince of the world was coming, but Satan had nothing in Jesus' life on which to lay claim (John 14:30). Jesus refused to surrender to sin.

OLD TESTAMENT PROPHECIES

At the beginning of this study, we looked at many of the Old Testament prophecies that would come to pass. Before we study the last days of Jesus, we need to review some of the prophecies that have to do with the betrayal, crucifixion, burial, resurrection, and ascension of the Savior. It is very important that we remember that nothing in Jesus' life happened by accident. Each detail was foreordained and known by Jesus Himself. Every action He took was planned and under His control.

As your teacher gives you verses from the Old Testament to look up, describe the New Testament situation that fulfilled each prophecy.

1. _____

2. _____

3. _____

4. _____

5. _____

6. _____

7. _____

8. _____

9. _____

10. _____

11. _____

12. _____

_____

13. _____

_____

JESUS FORETELLS HIS SUFFERINGS

Jesus' three-year ministry built to a climax—one that He planned. He spent His three years ministering to people, healing the sick, raising the dead, casting out demons, and teaching great truths that were new to the religious leaders of the time.

At first, only a few of the religious leaders began to hate Jesus. As Jesus performed more miracles and professed to be the true Son of God, more people began rejecting Him and responding with hatred. Finally, after the raising of Lazarus from the dead—a miracle that evidenced Christ's deity beyond all doubt—they hated Him even more. They had hardened their hearts and would not believe truth.

As we study these things, remember once again that Jesus is the One in control; nothing can or will happen that He and the Father have not planned and designed for a great purpose.

- Read each of the following passages and explain what Jesus actually said about His future and the things that would come to pass.

  - Mark 8:31; Luke 9:22 _____

    _____

    _____

  - John 3:14 _____

    _____

    _____

  - John 7:33; 13:33 _____

    _____

    _____

  - Matthew 17:22–23 _____

    _____

    _____

- Matthew 20:17–19 _____
  _____
  _____
  _____
  _____

- Luke 18:31–33 _____
  _____
  _____

- According to Luke 18:34, how did the disciples react to the things that Jesus told them and why? _____
  _____
  _____

People's hatred of Christ developed into a desire to kill Him. Many of the common people were still turning to Him, but many of the religious rulers had hardened their hearts against Him. They believed that in order to maintain authority over the people they must remove Jesus. Their hardened hearts had silenced even their consciences. Not only did they plan to kill Jesus, but they also justified their plan by reasoning that they were actually "saving" Israel.

With such distorted reasoning, they wasted no time plotting how to kill Jesus. Though no one knew the exact beginning of His final hours except Jesus, they were getting close. Because people did not know the timing, many did not believe these events would actually take place. They should have understood, but they didn't. Many times Jesus had told His disciples what was to take place. Jesus foretold His sufferings time and time again, and the prophets had explained these things many years before. Now the fullness of the time was come (Gal. 4:4).

IMPORTANT PLACES IN JESUS' MINISTRY

- Locate the places discussed below. Write each number by the appropriate dot on the map.

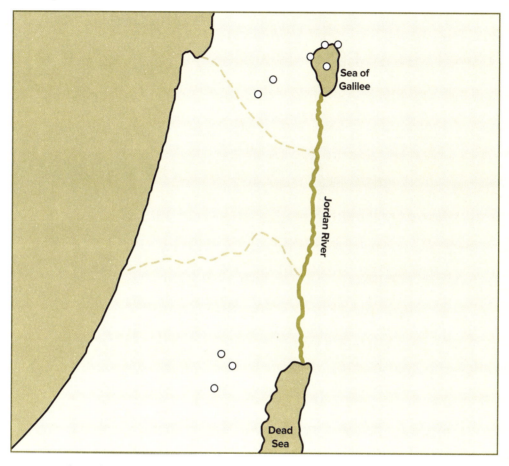

1. Where the Sermon on the Mount was given, and the apostles were ordained
2. Jerusalem (where Jesus attended the Passover)
3. Capernaum (where Jesus did many miracles)
4. A great storm was quieted here
5. Bethsaida (where 5,000 were fed)
6. Bethany (where Lazarus, Mary, and Martha lived)
7. Nazareth (where Jesus grew up)
8. Bethlehem (where Jesus was born)
9. Cana (where Jesus performed His first miracle)

MY RELATIONSHIP TO CHRIST

Review the major prophecies of the Old Testament concerning Jesus, and study how God perfectly brought those things to pass in Jesus' birth, life, death, and resurrection, despite opposing circumstances and people. Write a composition showing how God controlled and managed problems that could have interfered with His will for Jesus.

TEACHER'S LESSON NOTES

INVISIBLE FORCES

- _____ and powers
- Rulers of the _____ of this world
- Spiritual wickedness in _____

THE WORK AND POWER OF SATAN

- Blinds _____ of unbelievers
- Power to deceive with _____ and _____
- _____ upon men

CHRIST THE VICTOR

- Satan has no part of _____
- Jesus cast out the _____ of this world
- Jesus destroyed the _____ of Satan
- Jesus _____ us from and _____ the power of Satan

WE MUST RESIST SATAN

- _____ to God
- _____ the Devil
- Don't follow those who _____
- Stand strong in your _____
- Put on the full _____ of God
- Use the _____ of God to defeat Satan

THE TRIUMPHAL ENTRY

In Lesson 24, we studied the raising of Lazarus from the dead. This miracle had a great effect on many people. According to John 11:45, most of those who saw this evidence that Jesus was truly the Messiah believed on Him. But we also notice in verse 46 that "some of them went their ways to the Pharisees, and told them what things Jesus had done."

SCENE ONE

The Religious Leaders Meet:

- The religious leaders face a difficult problem. Discuss the various aspects of their problem according to John 11:47–48._____

_____

_____

_____

_____

_____

Caiaphas Solves the Problem:

- Joseph Caiaphas was appointed high priest in A. D. 25 and has therefore watched the ministry of Jesus from the very beginning. Based on verses 49–50, how does he say they should deal with the problems that have been raised? _____

_____

_____

_____

_____

- John, in writing his Gospel, expounded on what Caiaphas had resolved in verses 51–52. How did Caiaphas unwittingly play into the hands of God? _____

  _____

  _____

  _____

- Finally, at the end of the scenario, what decision had been made? See both verse 53 and verse 57. _____

  _____

  _____

  _____

SCENE TWO

Jesus, knowing what is to happen in the following week, continues to control the situation by first going to Ephraim, which is about twenty miles northeast of Jerusalem. According to John 11:54, Jesus no longer wanted to be openly seen among the Jews. He did not want the divine plan to be altered in any way. It was now close to the time of the Passover, and many of the Jews were going to Jerusalem early in order to purify themselves before the Passover. They were looking for Jesus and wondered if He would be there.

- Then, six days before the Passover, Jesus arrives in Bethany once again. Compare Matthew 26:6–13 with John 12:1–8 and explain the details of what happened at the supper. Include where the supper was held, who came to Jesus with ointment, why certain people were indignant, and how Jesus responded to their feelings.

  _____

  _____

  _____

  _____

  _____

  _____

  _____

  _____

  _____

SCENE THREE

- This scene is in two parts. Read each of the following passages and explain what two attitudes are coming together.

    - John 12:9 _____
    _____
    _____
    _____

    - John 12:10–11 _____
    _____
    _____
    _____

SCENE FOUR

- Outline each step that was followed in as much detail as possible in preparation for the entry into Jerusalem on Sunday. Compare Matthew 21:1–7; Mark 11:1–7, and Luke 19:29–35. _____
    _____
    _____
    _____
    _____
    _____
    _____
    _____

- Why do you think Jesus rode a donkey into the city, rather than a horse or some other animal—or even enter by walking? (See Zech. 9:9.)_____
    _____
    _____

SCENE FIVE

- Jesus rides the donkey to the Mount of Olives and descends from there into the city of Jerusalem. As He descends, what begins to take place? (See Luke 19:36–38; John 12:12–13 and Mark 11:7–11.) _____

  _____

  _____

  _____

  _____

  _____

  _____

- The Pharisees are again present to watch each detail of what is happening to Jesus. According to Luke 19:39–40, what takes place between them and Jesus?

  _____

  _____

  _____

- In Luke 19:41–44, we see that as Jesus beheld the city of Jerusalem, He began to weep. Why was He weeping? _____

  _____

Never before in His earthly life had Jesus permitted such a demonstration as during His triumphal entry into Jerusalem. He clearly foresaw the result of what was happening. It would bring Him to the cross. The events connected with this triumphant ride would be the talk of the town in Jerusalem for the Passover. The religious leaders, seeing the effect He had on the people, would want to get rid of Him quickly. He knew also that after His crucifixion many would remember these events in connection with His trial, death, and resurrection. They would search the prophecies and be convinced that Jesus was the Messiah and believe on Him for salvation.

THE PASSOVER CELEBRATION

- Jesus arrived in Jerusalem at the time of the Passover feast, which would take place in just a few days. Explain the purpose of the Passover celebration for the Jews and why Jesus was to be crucified at this particular time. _____

  _____

  _____

  _____

  _____

  _____

  _____

MY RELATIONSHIP TO CHRIST

At this point in Christ's ministry, everyone around Him had to make a decision about who He is and what He had said. Some people hardened their hearts and responded in hatred and unbelief. Some people believed His words and loved and worshipped Him.

- Discuss an area in your life or in the world in which you are faced with a similar decision—that is, where a blindness or hardness of heart is apparent or could develop, and how you will respond. _____

  _____

  _____

  _____

  _____

  _____

  _____

TEACHER'S LESSON NOTES

A HARD OR TENDER HEART?

_____ (Luke 16:14–15)

- _____

- _____

_____ (Luke 19:1–10)

- Recognized _____

- Recognized _____

_____ (Luke 16:19–31)

_____ (Luke 16:19–31)

DAYS OF CONFLICT

- Jesus observed a fig tree as He walked toward Jerusalem the next day. Mark 11:12–14 describes the incident. As Jesus approached the fig tree, what was He looking for, and what did He find instead? _____

  _____

Jesus used this tree to illustrate an important attitude that was being displayed toward Him. In the Old Testament, the fig tree is used to symbolize Israel as a nation. It is obvious from the attitude of the religious leaders that Israel, instead of bringing forth fruit and believing in the Messiah, was rejecting Him.

- What condemnation did Jesus pronounce on the fig tree because of this, and what did the disciples notice immediately? See Matthew 21:18–21. _____

  _____

  _____

THE FIRST CONFLICT: CLEANSING THE TEMPLE

In the first year of Christ's ministry, Jesus had cleansed the temple in Jerusalem of those who would use it for purposes other than honoring and praising God. This took place at the time of the Passover, and once again it is Passover time. Many had come to the temple to sell animals and other wares to use in the sacrifices and feasting during the Passover. Moneychangers were also there to provide their services for those who desired to buy and sell.

- Read Matthew 21:12–14 and describe what took place when Jesus again went into the temple. _____

  _____

  _____

  _____

_____

_____

_____

In Matthew 21:15–16, the chief priests and scribes noted what was happening. They were very upset because they were receiving some of the money from the sales that were going on in the temple.

- How did Jesus respond to them in verse 17? _____

_____

THE SECOND CONFLICT: QUESTIONING JESUS' AUTHORITY

The incident with the fig tree and the cleansing of the temple took place on Monday of Jesus' last week on Earth. Tuesday of the final week was a day in which Jesus silenced His critics and sealed His fate. The first group that came to Him in the court of the temple was the chief priests and the elders.

- What specifically did they say to Jesus in Matthew 21:23? _____

_____

_____

They would not have believed Him if He had told them that His authority was the authority of God, so He asked them a question. He said that if they answered His question, He would answer theirs. Then He asked whether the ministry of John the Baptist was from heaven or from men. These religious leaders would not answer because they knew that if they said it was from heaven, Jesus would ask them why they did not believe what John said about Him. If they said it was from men, they were afraid of what the people would do to them because the people considered John to be a prophet.

Then Jesus taught three parables to warn them of the price they would pay for rejection of Him as the Messiah. Briefly explain each parable and try to explain the meaning behind the parable.

Matthew	The Parable	The Meaning
21:28–32		
21:33–46		
22:1–10		

Now when the chief priests and the Pharisees understood that these parables were talking about them, they tried to take Jesus; but they were afraid to do so because of the multitude.

THE THIRD CONFLICT: QUESTIONS TO ENTRAP JESUS

The religious leaders grew concerned over Jesus' popularity, boldness in the temple, and healing the sick. They constantly held meetings, trying to find a legal way to arrest Jesus and declare Him guilty. They wanted Him dead before the Passover supper on Thursday evening. This was Tuesday. They knew they must act fast.

As Jesus was in the temple teaching, the Pharisees first confronted His authority. They asked three more questions, hoping to trick Him into giving an answer that they could use to convict Him. Below are the three questions. Read the complete passage and indicate how Jesus showed divine wisdom in the way He answered each question.

Question One: Is it lawful to pay taxes to Caesar? This question was asked by spies of the Pharisees who had been sent out to trap Jesus. They tried to pose as common people who were followers of Jesus when they first flattered Him by saying, "Master, we know that thou art true, and teachest the way of God in truth . . . ." (See Matthew 22:15–22.)

- What was Jesus' answer to their question? (22:21) _____
  _____
  _____

- How did they respond to Jesus' answer? (22:22) _____
  _____

Question Two: A woman had married seven brothers in turn. They asked, "in the resurrection, whose wife will she be?"

- What was Jesus' answer? (See Matthew 22:23–33.) _____
  _____
  _____
  _____
  _____
  _____

- How did they respond to Jesus' answer? (22:33) _____
  _____

Question Three: "Master, which is the great commandment in the law?" This question which was often disputed among the religious leaders themselves was asked by a scribe.

- What was Jesus' answer? (See Matthew 22:36–40.) _____

  _____

  _____

  _____

  _____

CHRIST'S UNANSWERABLE QUESTION

- Jesus proposed His own question to the Pharisees in Matthew 22:41–45. What was it? _____

- According to Matthew 22:46, what response did Jesus receive?_____

  _____

  _____

MY RELATIONSHIP TO CHRIST

One of the most important aspects of becoming a mature young person is being able to take a stand for what is right, no matter what the outward circumstances. God definitely wants us to learn to make decisions and consistently follow through with what is right. Think about each of the following areas of your life and consider what decisions you must be willing to make in each area.

- My Relationship to God: _____

  _____

  _____

- My Relationship to My Family: _____

  _____

  _____

- Dealing with My Friends: _____

  _____

  _____

- Considering My Future: _____

_____

_____

TEACHER'S LESSON NOTES

MOSES

- "I have set before you _____ and _____, _____ and _____: therefore, choose _____." (Deut. 30:19)

JOSHUA

- "_____ you this day whom ye will _____." (Josh. 24:15)

ELIJAH

- "How long halt ye between _____?" (1 Kings 18:21)

A WARNING

- "A _____ man is _____ in all his ways." (James 1:8)

FINAL WARNINGS

It was the last day of Christ's teaching in the temple. Throngs of people had been attracted to Him. They crowded the temple and listened closely to His words. The situation was very strange indeed, for people were accustomed to listening to their religious leaders who wore beautiful robes and garments, who seemed pious and religious, and who talked from an exalted position. Jesus was different. He wore the clothing of a common person, and yet He had the dignity of a king. Jesus was calm and spoke with great authority.

THE MOTIVES OF THE RELIGIOUS LEADERS

The religious leaders had rejected Jesus and His teachings and continually condemned Him and tried to ensnare Him in order to persecute Him. But they had done so in vain, for Jesus had an answer for every question; and all His answers had the authority of God.

Jesus had told parables and given warnings to try to awaken the Pharisees and the other religious leaders to the truth of who He was. Though warnings had been given, they went unheeded, for these men would not listen. Now Jesus knows the time for the cross is at hand. No longer does He use subtleties to teach; now He speaks clearly and forcefully of the corruption that He saw. Before He went to the cross, He wanted to fully expose once and for all the inner character of the priests, rulers, and Pharisees.

As you read and think through the following passages, note how Jesus referred to these men, what He condemned them for doing, and then explain what their inner motives were. All passages are from Matthew 23.

Matthew 23	What Did Jesus Call Them?	What Did Jesus Condemn Them for Doing?	What Were Their Inner Motives?
2–4			
5–7			
13–15			
23–24			
25–28			

THE WIDOW'S MITE

It was at this point that Jesus noticed a widow who was giving an offering to the Lord. Read Mark 12:41–44 and answer the following questions about this incident.

- What attitude did the widow seem to have as she approached the place of offering?

  _____

  _____

- What do you think her status and position in life were? _____

  _____

- What did Jesus point out about her inner motives? _____

  _____

  _____

It is your motive that gives character to all your actions, stamping them with hypocrisy or with moral worth. God does not necessarily praise those things that we consider important. God notices those things done with an attitude of love and dependence on Him. A heart of faith and love is much dearer to God than the most costly gift. The widow gave the little she had. And she gave in faith, believing that God would not overlook her need. It was her unselfish spirit and faith that God would bless.

GREEKS WHO WISHED TO SEE JESUS

Jesus had left the temple as one who had finished His task. He had said what was necessary to expose once and for all the hypocrisy of those who profess religion but were far from God. As He left the temple, some others approached Him. Read John 12:20–43 to find the following answers.

- Who wanted to see Jesus? (12:20–22) _____

  _____

- These men were not Jews, but Gentiles. What did Jesus do rather than talk openly with these men according to verse 36? _____

- Obviously, this was not the normal reaction of Jesus to those who came to Him. Jesus must have had a reason for doing this. Read verses 23, 27, and 32–33 and explain why Jesus did not greet these men at this time. _____

  _____

  _____

  _____

- However, some Jewish leaders did believe in Him. According to 12:42–43, why would they not admit this openly? _____

  _____

  _____

- What inner problem do you think they still had? _____

  _____

THE FINAL PLOT

While these events were taking place and Jesus was delivering His final public messages, other important events were taking place. Jesus was fully aware of these "behind the scenes" happenings, as they were all a part of the great plan of salvation that was to take place. Though His opponents met in secret, Jesus was fulfilling His mission openly and without hypocrisy.

As you read the following verses, explain who is plotting against Jesus and what they are plotting to do.

Matthew	Who Is Meeting?	What Is Their Purpose?
26:1–4		
26:14–16		

MY RELATIONSHIP TO CHRIST

Jesus always looks for the inner motive behind what a person does. He exposes selfish and vain motives and attitudes. Acting religious outwardly does not necessarily mean that we are right in our hearts. Think of two areas in which teenagers can have wrong motives and attitudes, even though they are doing the right thing outwardly. Be ready to share these two areas with your class.

- First area: _____

  _____

- Second area: _____

  _____

TEACHER'S LESSON NOTES

SIGNS OF THE END OF THE AGE

- False _____ and false _____ (4:4–5, 23–27)

- _____ and _____ of wars (24:6–7)

- _____ and _____ (24:7)

- _____ (24:9–14)

THE TIME OF THE END

- No one knows but the _____ (24:36–44)

- We must be _____ (24:44)

LESSONS FROM THREE PARABLES

The Ten Virgins (25:1–13)

- "Be _____ for the coming of the Lord"

- _____ is a symbol of the Holy Spirit

The Talents (25:14–30)

- Let _____ use you

- Understand the principle of _____ and _____

- For those who reject Christ there will be _____, _____, and _____

The Sheep and the Goats (25:31–46)

- The Christian life involves _____

- Jesus' judgment of us will result in either eternal _____ or eternal _____

THE LAST PASSOVER

It was Passover Day. For over 1,000 years, the Jews had celebrated this special event. For over 1,000 years, God's people had remembered when they had been freed from bondage in Egypt. For over 1,000 years, they had remembered the last night of bondage in Egypt when the blood of a lamb over their doorposts had saved their firstborn from death. For over 1,000 years, they had sacrificed the blood of a lamb in celebration of God's goodness.

During each year of Jesus' life, He too had celebrated Passover. The Lamb of God would replace the need for a sacrificial lamb to be offered each year for the sins of the people. With this knowledge, Jesus asked His disciples to prepare for the Passover feast. Even in this, Jesus showed His foreknowledge of events and His control over what was about to happen.

- Read Luke 22:7–14 and explain the preparation events. _____

  _____

  _____

  _____

  _____

  _____

  _____

  _____

  _____

THE FIRST LORD'S SUPPER

The twelve disciples were meeting with Jesus in this upper chamber that Christ had previously told them to find. They were gathered to celebrate the Passover.

- What did Jesus tell them about this particular Passover celebration according to Luke 22:14–16? _____

  _____

  _____

  _____

- Now read Luke 22:17–20 and explain the pattern of the Lord's Supper as Jesus instituted it that night. Include the meaning of the symbols as Jesus explained them._____

  _____

  _____

  _____

  _____

  _____

A SERVANT OF SERVANTS

Many emotions and feelings were involved in this particular evening, and there was also a great deal of concern and bewilderment over this event. First, there was strife among the disciples.

- What was the problem, and how did Jesus answer them? (Luke 22:24–30)

  _____

  _____

  _____

  _____

At a feast such as this, it was customary for a servant to wash the feet of the guests; and on this occasion preparation had been made for this purpose. The pitcher, the basin, and the towel were there in readiness for the foot washing; but no servant was present. It was the disciples' place to perform this duty. But at this point none of the disciples was ready to accept the role of a servant. By their attitudes, they showed they were unwilling to humble themselves in such a manner. How sad that such feelings were evident during such an important time in Jesus' life!

- How would Christ respond? How could He show that true humility was the sign of true greatness? Read John 13:4–10 and answer the following.

    - What did Jesus do? _____

      _____

      _____

    - How did Peter respond to this? _____

      _____

    - How did Jesus answer Peter? _____

      _____

      _____

    - What was Peter's response? _____

      _____

    - What lessons do you think Jesus taught the disciples through this situation?

      _____

      _____

      _____

THREE PREDICTIONS

The Betrayal Foretold

- While they were sitting at the Passover table, Judas was full of thoughts of his own plans even while he was eating the symbols of Christ's broken body and shed blood. What did Jesus say one of His disciples would do? (John 13:21–30)?

  _____

- How did the other disciples respond to this? _____

  _____

  _____

  _____

- How did Jesus indicate the one who would betray Him, and what was the last statement that Jesus made to Judas? _____

  _____

  _____

  _____

- According to these same verses, who had taken control of Judas at this time?

  _____

The disciples probably still did not completely understand what had taken place. Since Judas was their treasurer, they may have assumed that Jesus had sent him on an errand. Remember that Judas had been a close part of their company for three years, and he had done nothing in their eyes to give them cause to suspect his motives. That same night, however, they would see the full impact of Jesus' words.

Peter's Denial Foretold

In John 13:37, Peter asked the Lord why he couldn't follow Him now. To show his great love for his Lord, he said that he would willingly lay down his life for Jesus.

- What had Jesus discussed in verse 31–36 that caused Peter to say these things?

  _____

  _____

  _____

  _____

- How did Jesus respond to Peter? What prediction did He make in verse 38?

  _____

  _____

- Peter responded to Jesus' prediction. What final words did Peter and the other disciples say about this in Mark 14:30–31? _____

  _____

  _____

Grief Will Turn into Joy

Jesus understood the confusion and feelings that the disciples were going through. He had just said that Judas was ready to betray Him and that Peter would deny Him. The disciples knew that something great and profound was about to happen, but they still did not fully understand.

- Knowing the grief that was to come for each of them, what assurance did Jesus give them about the future? (John 14:1–4) _____

  _____

  _____

  _____

  _____

MY RELATIONSHIP TO CHRIST

When we read of Peter and Judas, we cannot imagine that we would either deny or betray Jesus. But we don't realize how much of life is involved in denials and betrayals. Jesus came to die on the cross for those types of sins that we commit.

- Write a short paragraph explaining how you yourself are sometimes guilty of these sins. _____

  _____

  _____

  _____

  _____

  _____

TEACHER'S LESSON NOTES

WHEN IT WAS BEGUN

- The night of the _____

- In the upper room with _____ and His _____

NAMES OF THE CELEBRATION

• _____

• _____

REPLACING THE PASSOVER CELEBRATION

• Jesus became the sacrificial _____

• Jesus shed His _____ on the cross

THE PURPOSE OF THE LORD'S SUPPER

• Celebrated in _____ of Jesus

• The bread: symbol of Jesus' _____

• The wine: symbol of Jesus' _____

• A pledge of Jesus' _____

• Are not to be taken _____

LAST WORDS AND PROMISES

On the night that Jesus was to be betrayed, after He had shared the first Communion with His disciples, Jesus spoke to them, teaching them essential lessons for life and the future.

A NEW COMMANDMENT

The Jews had rejected Jesus completely. As we have seen, Jesus had gathered His own around Him and shared a special new meal with them. Now He spent some time telling them many secrets before He departed from them. He wanted to comfort His disciples, for He knew how hard it would be for them when He was gone. They would be like sheep without a shepherd. This little group of men, though they were not highly thought of in the world, were "His own." His last words to His disciples before His death are recorded in John 13–17.

It is wonderful that Jesus selected and loved men such as these, for they were very much the same type of people that we are. They were the kind of people who were closest to His heart.

And now, since announcing His going, the Lord began to speak intimately to this special group. First He told them that He was giving them "a new commandment."

- Read John 13:34–35 and explain the new commandment and its purpose.

  _____
  _____
  _____

- Copy John 15:12 and explain the importance of Jesus' words.

  _____
  _____
  _____
  _____
  _____

THE COMFORTER

The new commandment that Jesus had just given to the disciples seems at first easy to accomplish. But once we begin to think of the times we have been jealous, unkind, angry, or bitter against someone, then we recognize how difficult this commandment is to keep. Jesus knew that in and of ourselves, we would never be able to love one another as He loves us. That is why He began to teach His disciples about the coming of the Holy Spirit. It is the Holy Spirit who would live in each of us and give us the power to love one another. Read John 14:16–26 and list at least six promises that Jesus made concerning the Holy Spirit.

1. _____

2. _____

3. _____

4. _____

5. _____

6. _____

"I AM"

- In Exodus 3:14, God used this phrase for the first time. What were His words? To whom were they said? What were the circumstances?_____

  _____

  _____

  _____

- In John 8:58, Jesus used the same words to identify Himself. What did He say in this passage? How did He identify Himself?_____

  _____

  _____

- Jesus again used the phrase in Revelation 1:18. How did He use the phrase? How was He identifying Himself? _____

  _____

  _____

  _____

- In the Gospel of John, Jesus used this same phrase many times to describe Himself in various ways. Look up each verse and complete the phrase.

  - John 6:35 "I Am _____"

  - John 8:12 "I Am _____"

  - John 10:9 "I Am _____"

  - John 10:11 "I Am _____"

  - John 11:25 "I Am _____"

  - John 14:6 "I Am _____"

    - What does this statement mean? _____
    _____
    _____
    _____

  - John 15:1 "I Am _____"

    - What does this statement mean? _____
    _____
    _____
    _____

MY RELATIONSHIP TO CHRIST

Jesus began to talk even more intimately about how He would live His life in His disciples after the resurrection. Here Jesus truly revealed the real secret of the Christian life. Read John 15:1–16 by yourself or as a class.

- After discussing the passage as a class, try to explain in a paragraph of your own what Jesus is saying to you about how your life and His life are intertwined.

_____
_____
_____
_____
_____

TEACHER'S LESSON NOTES

JESUS PRAYED FOR _____ (JOHN 17:1–8)

The _____ work (17:4)

- The disciples _____ the Word

- The disciples _____ the Word

- The disciples _____ the Word

Two requests

- To be glorified in _____

- To be glorified in _____

JESUS PRAYED FOR _____ (17:7–9)

_____ them (17:11–12)

_____ them (17:17–19)

JESUS PRAYED FOR _____ (17:20–26)

That we may be _____ (17:21–23)

- In fellowship with the _____ and _____

- With _____

That we may be _____ (17:24)

BETRAYAL AND TRIALS

"The hour" had come! The greatest work of Christ on Earth remained to be done. He was to die so that He might glorify the Father and save a sinful world. Jesus left the upper room with eleven disciples to begin His work. In this lesson we will study scene by scene what happened on the night of His betrayal.

SCENE ONE: THE GARDEN OF GETHSEMANE

Jesus had been talking with His disciples all evening. Now, as He slowly made His way to the Garden of Gethsemane, He became quiet and thoughtful. He had often visited this spot for meditation and prayer, but never with a heart so full as on this night.

Study Mark 14:32–42 and answer the following questions.

- How did Jesus organize the disciples in the garden? _____
  _____
  _____
  _____

- How was Jesus feeling? _____
  _____

- How many times did Jesus return to find His disciples sleeping? _____

- How did Jesus explain why they slept? _____
  _____
  _____

- Why do you think the disciples could sleep so easily on such a night?
  _____
  _____

- What did Jesus pray for Himself? _____

  _____

  _____

- According to Luke 22:43–44, describe what else happened as He prayed.

  _____

  _____

- Finally, at the end of His prayer, what did Jesus say was about to happen? (Mark 14:42) _____

  _____

SCENE TWO: THE ARREST

- While Jesus and the disciples were in the olive grove, Judas, followed by soldiers and officials, came up to Jesus. Read Luke 22:47–53 and John 18:1–11. How did Judas identify Jesus? _____

  _____

- What was Jesus' attitude throughout His arrest? What remarks did He make that showed this attitude? _____

  _____

  _____

  _____

- Describe the last miracle Jesus performed. _____

  _____

- According to Matthew 26:56, how did the disciples react to His arrest?

  _____

SCENE THREE: THE RELIGIOUS TRIAL

Jesus was brought before two men and a religious group at three different times during the night.

- According to John 18:12–13, where was Jesus taken first? _____

    _____

    _____

- According to John 18:19–21, Jesus was obviously in perfect control before Annas. What was He asked to explain? _____

    _____

- How did Jesus respond? _____

    _____

    _____

    _____

- Why was Jesus able to be in control of this situation? _____

    _____

    _____

- What happened next according to John 18:22–23? _____

    _____

- How did Jesus respond? _____

    _____

- According to John 18:24, where was Jesus taken next? _____

    _____

- At the home of Caiaphas, the high priest, with the Sanhedrin in attendance, they tried another tactic. According to Matthew 26:59–60, what did they try to do, and did it work? _____

    _____

    _____

- According to Matthew 26:60–63, who came forward, and what charge was finally made against Jesus? _____

    _____

    _____

- How did Jesus respond? _____

- Finally, in Matthew 26:64, Jesus spoke. How did He answer these men?

  _____

  _____

  _____

- What events took place next according to Matthew 26:65–68 and 27:1–2?

  _____

  _____

  _____

SCENE FOUR: THE POLITICAL TRIALS

Jesus was taken before Pilate, the Roman governor of Judea.

Verses	What Did the Opposition Do or Say?	How Did Jesus Respond?
Mark 15:2		
Mark 15:3		
Mark 15:4–5		
Luke 23:2, 5		
Luke 23:4		

Luke 23:6–7 explains that Pilate then asked Jesus if He was a Galilean. When Pilate found that He was, he recognized that this case was technically out of his jurisdiction. Jesus was really under the jurisdiction of Herod, so Pilate sent Jesus to see him. Pilate thought it fortunate that Herod was visiting Jerusalem at the time.

Verses	What Did the Opposition Do or Say?	How Did Jesus Respond?
Luke 23:8–9		
Luke 23:10		
Luke 23:11		

- Study Luke 23:13–25 and Matthew 27:24 and answer the following questions.

  - What did Pilate think? _____

    _____

  - What did the people think? _____

    _____

  - What did Pilate want? _____

  - What did the people want? _____

    _____

  - What did Pilate finally do? _____

    _____

    _____

  - Why do you think Pilate decided to do this? _____

    _____

    - _____

WHAT HAPPENED TO JUDAS?

- Judas finally realized what he had done when he saw the results of his betrayal. Read the story of what happened in Matthew 27:3–10 and answer the following in your own words.

    - What did Judas do with the silver he had been given in exchange for betraying Jesus? _____

      _____

    - What response did he get from the Jewish leaders? _____

      _____

    - What did Judas do then? _____

      _____

    - What did the chief priests do with the silver? _____

      _____

CHRIST'S FINAL NIGHT

Jerusalem was both the religious and the political capital of Israel. Here were the palaces of Herod and Pilate, the political leaders. Here also were the Jewish temple and the Jewish spiritual leaders. Both of the groups wanted Jesus Christ to die on the cross.

Trace the route along which Jesus was taken during the night before the crucifixion and write the following numbers on the appropriate places on the map of Jerusalem.

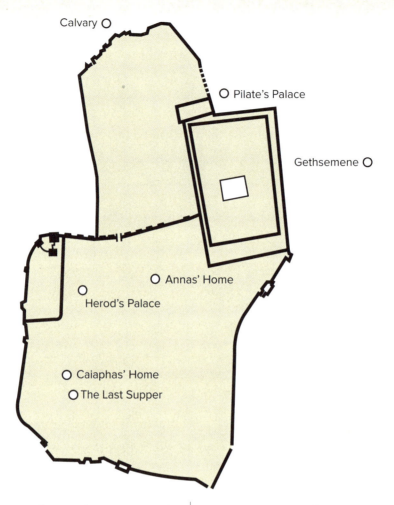

Calvary O

O Pilate's Palace

Gethsemene O

O Annas' Home

O
Herod's Palace

O Caiaphas' Home
O The Last Supper

1. Jesus arrived from Bethany to enjoy the last Passover supper with His disciples. Here He instituted the new ordinance that we know as Communion or the Lord's Supper. This is where the upper room was found.

2. After Judas left, Jesus and the rest of the disciples went to the Garden of Gethsemane, where Jesus prayed and the disciples slept. It was in this garden that Jesus was betrayed by Judas and taken captive.

3. Jesus was taken to the home of Annas, the former high priest and father-in-law of the current high priest, Caiaphas.

4. Jesus was taken before the religious council at the home of Caiaphas.

5. Jesus was taken to the judgment hall in Pilate's palace.

6. Pilate sent Jesus to Herod's palace.

7. Herod sent Jesus back to Pilate, where He was finally judged and received a sentence of death by crucifixion.

8. Jesus was finally taken to Golgotha (Calvary), where He was crucified.

MY RELATIONSHIP TO CHRIST

Both Judas and Peter were tested. The difference between the two men was that Peter truly loved the Lord and believed in Him for salvation while Judas did not. Judas deceived everyone except Jesus—only Jesus knew his true character. Peter was not trying to be deceptive, but he did not understand his own heart.

Jesus showed both men what was in their hearts. Judas realized his guilt and hanged himself. Peter saw the truth about himself and became a better disciple because of the testing.

In the Book of Acts, we see how the power of God worked in Peter's life so that he became a great preacher and led many people to salvation. There will also be times when you will be tested. The Lord knows what is in your heart, and He wants you to know these things also so that you can grow and mature into a strong person who can make wise decisions.

- Discuss below a time when you were tested. How did you respond? What did you learn about yourself? What have you learned about yourself that can help you grow and mature into a better Christian? _____

  _____

  _____

  _____

  _____

  _____

  _____

  _____

TEACHER'S LESSON NOTES

PURPOSE—TO _____ OUR HEARTS

METHODS

- Demanding _____

- Leading in a _____ path

- Giving opportunities to _____

- Giving difficult _____

- Permitting _____

- Allowing _____

EXAMPLE—_____

- Denied Christ by the _____

- Denied Christ at the _____

- Denied Christ at the _____ again with _____ and _____

- Saw _____ and _____ bitterly

THE DAY CHRIST DIED

Pilate did not think that Jesus was guilty or that He deserved to die. He had tried to free Jesus by giving the people a choice between Jesus and Barabbas. But the people chose Barabbas—an infamous criminal. They wanted Jesus to be crucified. Finally, Pilate sentenced Jesus to die by crucifixion, as they wanted. So Jesus was led away with the cross. We must remember that Jesus had just been through a night of torture. He had been beaten and marred beyond recognition and therefore could not carry the weight of the cross by Himself.

- How did the soldiers deal with this situation according to Luke 23:26?

  _____

  _____

- As Jesus, along with Simon, found their way toward Golgotha, who came with Him, and how did Jesus respond to them? (Luke 23:27–31)_____

  _____

  _____

  _____

  _____

- Read Matthew 27:33–38 and explain what happened once they arrived at Golgotha.

  _____

  _____

  _____

  _____

  _____

  _____

How did Jesus respond to these things? One way we can learn about Jesus' response is by studying the words He spoke while on the cross.

JESUS' FIRST STATEMENT (LUKE 23:34)

• What was Jesus' first statement? _____

_____

• What do you think Jesus meant when He said, "They know not what they do"?

_____

_____

• Some of the people who were watching began to mock Jesus. What kinds of things did they say to Him according to Matthew 27:39–43? _____

_____

_____

_____

_____

_____

_____

_____

_____

_____

JESUS' SECOND STATEMENT (LUKE 23:43)

• According to Luke 23:39, one of the thieves that was crucified along with Jesus was also mocking Jesus. What did he say? _____

_____

• The other thief had a completely different attitude. What did he say to the thief? (Luke 23:40–41) _____

_____

_____

• Then what did he say to Jesus? (23:42)_____

_____

• How did Jesus respond to this thief? (23:43) _____

_____

JESUS' THIRD STATEMENT (JOHN 19:26–27)

- Jesus looked down from the cross and saw several people that had been very close to Him through the years of His ministry. Who were these people? (John 19:25–26)

  _____

  _____

  _____

- What did Jesus say to His mother? (John 19:26) _____

- What did Jesus say to John? (John 19:27)_____

- What was Jesus' purpose in saying these words? _____

  _____

JESUS' FOURTH STATEMENT (MATT. 27:46)

- Read Matthew 27:45–47 and explain what remarkable occurrence took place during the middle of the day (from 12 noon to 3:00 PM). _____

  _____

- Jesus cried out during this time, but many of those who heard Him thought He was calling out to Elijah to save Him. What did Jesus really cry out?_____

  _____

JESUS' FIFTH STATEMENT (JOHN 19:28)

- After Jesus cried out, He expressed a personal need. What did He say?

  _____

- What happened next? (John 19:29–30a) _____

  _____

As soon as this had taken place, Jesus made two more statements.

JESUS' SIXTH STATEMENT (JOHN 19:30)

- What was this statement? _____

- Meaning and significance of this statement: _____

  _____

  _____

  _____

JESUS' SEVENTH STATEMENT (LUKE 23:46)

- What was this statement? _____

  _____

- Meaning and significance of this statement: _____

  _____

  _____

- At the time of Christ's death, many supernatural events took place that confounded all who saw them. Read Matthew 27:51–54 and list the miracles that happened.

  _____

  _____

  _____

  _____

  _____

  _____

MY RELATIONSHIP TO CHRIST

- Of all the events and incidents that took place on this day of days, what details had the greatest impact on you? Why? _____

  _____

  _____

  _____

  _____

  _____

THE RESURRECTION

The greatest day of history is finally over. People who began the day watching a great spectacle and jeering at the "King of the Jews" ended their day in awe and even terror as they contemplated all that they had seen. Many had gone home to think about these things. The Jewish leaders were anxious to get Jesus down from the cross before the beginning of the Jewish Sabbath. They also wanted to be done with the whole business so everyone could begin to forget about what had taken place.

THE BURIAL

But many people will be interested to know what happened next. Pretend you are a reporter for a Jewish newspaper, and you have stayed behind to learn the rest of the story. You want to examine every angle and get every thread of information for your readers.

Research the following passages for information for your news story: Matthew 27:57–66; Mark 15:42–47; Luke 23:50–56 and John 19:38–42. Begin by answering the following questions.

- Who went to Pilate to ask for Jesus' body? _____

- What position did this man hold? _____
  _____

- Why was he a "secret disciple" of Jesus? _____
  _____

- What did Pilate do to make sure that Jesus was dead? _____
  _____

- Who helped him by bringing spices for Jesus' body? _____

- In what did they wrap Jesus' body? _____

- In whose tomb was Jesus laid? _____

- How do we know this tomb was new? _____
  _____

- Who watched to see where the body was buried? _____
  _____

- What request did the Jewish leaders make to Pilate? _____
  _____

- Why did they make this request? _____
  _____

Now write your own news story based on the facts you have collected. Write a headline that captures the attention of your readers. Use an opening sentence that brings out the key ideas. Then give the details of your story in the proper sequence of events.

ZION GAZETTE

Jerusalem, Israel   April • 30 AD

_____

_____
(Headline)

_____	_____
_____	_____
_____	_____
_____	_____
_____	_____
_____	_____
_____	_____
_____	_____
_____	_____

Jesus was convicted because He said He was the king of the Jews and the Messiah. In other words, Jesus claimed to be God. To the Jews, this was blasphemy. Though He told the truth, He was accused of treason. Jesus was definitely a king but not the kind of king that the people, or even the disciples, expected.

- What kind of king was Jesus, and what is His kingdom? What did the people and the disciples expect of Him as their king? _____
_____
_____

- The impossible had happened, and the disciples could not understand the events that had taken place. Put yourself in the disciples' place. They were discouraged and greatly depressed. How would you have responded to seeing Jesus put to death? Would you have still believed that Jesus was the king and the Messiah?
_____
_____
_____
_____
_____

EASTER SUNDAY

The night of the Sabbath had slowly come to an end. Christ was still the prisoner of His tomb. The great stone was in its place; the Roman seal was unbroken; the guards were keeping their watch. Early in the morning, two of the women came to the tomb. They were bringing precious spices to anoint the Savior's body, for they were not considering His prophecy that He would rise from the dead.

- As they approached the tomb, they were very startled at what had taken place. Describe what happened according to Matthew 28:1–7.
_____
_____
_____
_____
_____

_____

_____

- The soldiers who had been guarding the tomb rushed into the city to tell what happened. What reward and orders were they now given? (Matt. 28:11–15)

_____

_____

_____

_____

- Why were they told to lie? What do you think the chief priests were afraid of?

_____

_____

_____

JESUS' APPEARANCES AFTER THE RESURRECTION

There are many who do not believe in the resurrection of Jesus Christ. They believe that Christ lived and that He was a great man, even a prophet. They may also believe that He should not have been crucified, for He was not guilty of anything. But they refuse to believe that He was resurrected from the dead.

It is important then to see how many times Christ showed Himself alive to those who knew He had died. The fact of His death is certain—and the fact that He arose from the dead is just as certain. As you read the following verses, find out to whom Jesus appeared after His resurrection and what the responses were.

Verses	Person(s)	Response to Jesus
Matthew 28:8–10		
Mark 16:9–11		

Luke 24:13–32		
Luke 24:34		
John 20:19–25		
John 20:26–29		
John 21:1–14		
Matthew 28:16–20		
1 Corinthians 15:6		
1 Corinthians 15:7		
Acts 1:4–9		
1 Corinthians 15:8		

MY RELATIONSHIP TO CHRIST

Though Jesus had told them that He would die and then be raised from the dead, the disciples did not really understand the truth of His words. The crucifixion had taken place, and the disciples had scattered in confusion and depression. No one was more surprised than the disciples to hear reports that the man who had died on the cross was walking around on Sunday. It was unbelievable—until He appeared before them, and they could deny it no longer.

- Suppose you had been one of the disciples. What would it have taken for you to believe that Jesus was alive? What makes you believe it now?

  _____

  _____

  _____

  _____

  _____

TEACHER'S LESSON NOTES

THE POWER OF CHRIST

- Demonstrated by _____

- Demonstrated by _____

- Is an _____ power

THE POWER OF CHRIST IN US

- Accompanies the _____

- Gives us _____ strength

THE ASCENSION

Jesus had spent forty days on the earth after the resurrection. During this time, the disciples, those closest to Him, and hundreds of others saw Jesus and talked to Him. There is no doubt that Jesus died on the cross, was buried, and rose again from the dead. Read Matthew 28:18–20 and Luke 24:46–49.

- According to these verses, what were some of Jesus' last words to His disciples?

  _____

  _____

  _____

  _____

  _____

  _____

THE LAST APPEARANCE

- Read Acts 1:4–14 and answer the following questions concerning the last appearance of Jesus. Describe what happened to Jesus the last time the disciples saw Him. Where is He now? _____

  _____

  _____

- List the promises made to the disciples both by Jesus and the angels.

  _____

  _____

  _____

  _____

  _____

- What did the disciples do after they witnessed this great event?

  _____

  _____

The lives of the disciples were changed forever. They began to speak openly and boldly about all they had seen. They were unafraid of consequences, for they knew they had the power of God to say these things. (Note particularly the power of God in Peter who before Jesus' death denied three times that he even knew Jesus.)

- Who boldly accused the "men of Israel" of killing "the Prince of life"? (Acts 3:12–15)

  _____

- What were the apostles given to help them bear witness to the resurrection? (Acts 4:33) _____

THE EXALTED POSITION OF CHRIST

Read each verse listed below and match it with the appropriate statement concerning the position of Christ today.

Mark 16:19	Hebrews 7:25	Philippians 2:9–11	1 Peter 3:22
Colossians 1:18	Revelation 5:12	Revelation 15:4	

- _____ Jesus now sits on the right hand of God.

- _____ All authority and power is given to Jesus, and all authorities arc subject to Him.

- _____ The name of Jesus is above every name. Every knee shall bow before Him, and every tongue shall confess that Jesus is Lord.

- _____ All nations shall worship before the Lord and glorify Him, for He alone is holy.

- _____ Jesus is head of the church and is preeminent in all things.

- _____ Jesus continually makes intercession for us.

- _____ Jesus alone is worthy to receive our praise.

NAMES AND TITLES OF CHRIST

In the very first lesson, we discussed some of the names given to Christ. Read the following verses and record the name or title for Christ used in each verse.

Scripture	Name or Title of Christ
Matthew 1:21	
Matthew 8:20	
Mark 1:24	
Luke 9:20	
John 1:1	
John 1:9	
John 8:58	
John 10:7	
John 11:25	
John 14:6	
John 15:1	
John 20:16	
Acts 7:52	
Acts 10:36	
1 Corinthians 2:8	
1 Corinthians 5:7	
1 Timothy 1:17	
1 Timothy 2:5	
Hebrews 5:9	
1 Peter 5:4	
Revelation 1:8	
Revelation 1:17	

MY RELATIONSHIP TO CHRIST

Choose one of the names of Christ that has particular meaning for your own life. State the name or title and explain what it means to you. _____

_____

_____

_____

_____

_____

TEACHER'S LESSON NOTES

A Place Prepared by _____

Built by _____

Contains a Register of _____

Has Room for All _____

Is a Place of Safe-keeping for _____

- Crown of _____

- Crown of _____

- Crown of _____

- _____ crown

Is a Place of Eternal _____

No more . . .

- _____

- _____

- _____

- _____

- _____

- _____

REVIEW

SHORT ANSWER

- Why did Jesus perform miracles? _____
  _____
  _____

- List the steps Jesus wants you to take if someone has offended you.
  _____
  _____

- What was the new commandment that Jesus gave to His disciples before His death?
  _____

- List some of the promises Christians have concerning the Holy Spirit.
  _____
  _____
  _____
  _____

- List at least 10 names or titles given to Christ in the Scriptures.
  _____
  _____
  _____
  _____
  _____

CHRONOLOGICAL ORDER

Number the following events in the order in which they occurred.

_____ Jesus is taken before Annas, Caiaphas, and the Sanhedrin.

_____ Jesus washes the feet of the disciples.

_____ Lazarus is raised from the dead.

_____ The disciples find the upper room as Jesus instructed.

_____ Jesus is tried before Pilate the first time.

_____ Jesus is taken to Golgotha and crucified between two thieves.

_____ Caiaphas proposes that Jesus be killed.

_____ Jesus overturns the moneychangers' tables in the temple.

_____ Jesus prays in the Garden of Gethsemane.

_____ Jesus is taken to Herod's palace.

_____ Jesus dies.

_____ Jesus is betrayed by a kiss for thirty pieces of silver.

_____ The disciples follow Jesus' directions and find the colt.

_____ Jesus ascends into heaven.

_____ Jesus rises from the dead the third day.

_____ Jesus is arrested by a band of soldiers.

_____ Pilate sentences Jesus to be crucified.

_____ Jesus enters Jerusalem.

_____ The veil in the temple is torn in two from top to bottom.

_____ Jesus is seen by the disciples and hundreds of others after His resurrection.

_____ Jesus is tried before Pilate the second time.

_____ Jesus speaks from the cross seven times.

WHO AM I?

A. Andrew	B. Pilate	C. Mary	D. Peter
E. Judas	F. John	G. Jesus	H. Holy Spirit
I. Children	J. Lazarus	K. Nicodemus	L. Barabbas
M. Caiaphas	N. Herod	O. Satan	P. Annas
Q. Thomas	R. James and John	S. Joseph of Arimathea	T. Philip and Andrew

	1.	The two disciples whose mother wanted these sons to sit on each side of Jesus in His kingdom
	2.	Jesus used them as an example to teach us how to develop a humble attitude
	3.	The "secret disciple" who asked Pilate for Jesus' body
	4.	His resurrection showed that Jesus will one day raise us all from the dead
	5.	A deceiver of man
	6.	The high priest
	7.	Anointed the feet of Jesus with costly ointments
	8.	Betrayed Jesus to the chief priests for thirty pieces of silver
	9.	Jesus foretold his denials
	10.	Washed the feet of the disciples
	11.	The Comforter
	12.	The head of all Jewish religious affairs; the father-in-law of Caiaphas
	13.	Pilate offered to release either this man or Jesus
	14.	He wanted to see a miracle when Jesus was brought before him
	15.	A Roman leader who could find no fault in Jesus
	16.	The disciple whom Jesus asked to take care of His mother
	17.	The disciple who refused to believe in Jesus' resurrection until he saw Jesus for himself

GROWING IN CHARACTER

The following is a list of many of the character qualities that have been discussed this year. For each trait, discuss areas of positive personal growth that have taken place in your life. Then explain areas that still need to be dealt with. You may not have something to write positively or negatively for every trait. As you do this, sincerely ask the Lord to show you your areas of strength and weakness.

Trait	Positive Growth	Areas to Work on
Integrity		
Faith		
Humility		
Obedience		
Submission		
Loyalty		
Courage		
Love		
Thankfulness		
Forgiveness		
Patience		
Positive Growth